PASS T

MO

HOW TO PASS THE MOT TEST
FIRST TIME EVERY YEAR

G000146739

VELOCE PUBLISHING PLC
PUBLISHERS OF FINE AUTOMOTIVE BOOKS

First published in 1994 by Veloce Publishing Plc., Godmanstone, Dorset DT2 7AE, England. Fax 0300 341065

ISBN 1 874105 35 9

Readers with ideas for automotive books, or books on other transport or related hobby subjects are invited to write to the editorial director of Veloce Publishing at the above address.

British Library Cataloguing in Publication Data -
A catalogue record for this book is available from the British Library.

Typesetting (Avant Garde, 10/11), design and page make-up all by Veloce on Apple Mac.

Printed and bound in England.

CONTENTS

PREFACE
ACKNOWLEDGEMENTS

The following companies provided useful help and/or information and photos for this book:

* Autoglass Ltd, PO Box 50, CLifton House, Goldington Road, Bedford, MK40 3YP. (0800 363636)

* Bendix Brakes Ltd., 19 Salisbury Road, Haydock Industrial Estate, St Helens, Merseyside, WA11 9XG. (0942 723828)

* Bailcast (Stickyboot), Chorley North Industrial Park, Chorley, Lancs, PR6 7BX. (0257 266060)

* Bilstein Shock Absorbers, Magard Ltd., 372 East Park Road, Leicester, LE5 5AY. (0533 730831)

* Black & Decker Ltd., West Point, The Grove, Slough, Berks, SL1 1QQ. (0753 511234)

* Gunson Ltd., Pudding Mill Lane, Stratford, London, E15 2PJ. (081 555 7421)

* Securon Ltd, Winchmore Hill, Amersham, Bucks, HP7 0NZ. (0494 434455)

* Sony Video, Sony House, South Street, Staines, Middx. TW18 4DF. (0784 467000)

* Sykes-Pickavant Tools Ltd., Warwick Works, Kilnhouse Lane, Lytham St Annes, Lancs, FY8 3DU. (0253 721291)

* Tar-Ox Brakes, GGB (Engineering Spares) ltd., 98 White Hart Lane, Wood Green, London, N22 5SG. (081 888 23545)

* Teng Tools, Tengvise Ltd., Unit 5, Flitwick Industrial Estate, Maulden Road, Flitwick, Beds, MK45 1UF. (0525 718080)

* Warco Benches, Warren Machine Tools (Guildford) Ltd, Warren Court, Middle Street, Shere, Surrey. (048 841 3434)

Many of the 'action' photos were taken at Halfords Service Centre, Northampton (0604 587094) and Mount Farm Motors, 2 Grove Ash, Dawson Road, Bletchley, Milton Keynes, MK1 1BZ (0908 377399). Particular thanks to Ivor Wheeler and Tim Smith at Halfords and Terry Lingwood and John Millward at Mount Farm Motors for their valuable time and information. Likewise The Motor Insurance Repair Research Centre for use of its diagrams. My thanks also to Sony (UK) Ltd., who provided a CCD-FX700E Hi-8 camcorder which was used as a video notebook and made collating facts and procedures so much easier.

Special thanks to Phil Blundell and Jeremy Redman of PMB Mobile Servicing (0908 504229/0374 290850), who were instrumental in the preparation of this book, providing skill, ingenuity and 'interesting' vehicles whenever required.

As ever, thanks to Ann for her patience in checking and collating.

All original diagrams by Davan Designs, PO Box 3, Blakesley, Northants, NN12 8DG. (0327 860742).

INTRODUCTION

This book covers cars and light commercial vehicles (up to 300 kgs gross weight) and various passenger carriers - basically, those vehicles which come under the heading of 'Class IV' - see the full listing later in this chapter. It encompasses around 90% of vehicles currently on UK roads.

The order in which the subject matter is approached is the same as listed in the *MoT Inspection Manual* - the MoT inspector's Bible. If it's good enough for them, it's good enough for us!

The MoT test was introduced in 1961, and was then little more than a cursory test of some of the car's basic features, notably steering, brakes and lights. Even then, it was only for vehicles over 10 years old.

It is now a much more comprehensive examination, though it has to be said, there are rather too many 'grey areas' for comfort, when it is considered that the aim of the test is to make sure that all vehicles on the road are safe; that's safe for the occupants and safe for other road users - me and you!

The rules are not there to penalise the majority, rather to weed out the *minority* who think it's OK to drive around in cars held together with bits of string, riding on leaking suspension units and braked by 5 year-old pads.

To many motorists, the annual MoT test ranks somewhere between bungey jumping from the Empire State building and being trapped in a lift with Jeremy Beadle. This fear, bordering on paranoia, goes some way to explain why every year, around half of the cars tested, fail.

❏ WHY SO MANY FAILURES?

By definition, some cars are absolute heaps and wouldn't pass in a month of Sundays. BUT they're the exception rather than the rule. In general, the reasons for failure can be boiled down to a) lack of preparation and a few simple checks or b) lack of knowledge about what the test entails or c) both!

The main problem is that motorists in general simply don't know what the testers will be testing and what the criteria are for pass and failure; if you don't know the rules, it makes playing the game more than a little difficult.

That's where this book comes in, for these pages contain everything you need to know in order to make sure your car passes first time, every time; testing and checking procedures, what is checked and (sometimes surprisingly) what isn't checked.

For the motorist with even modest DIY ability most of the pre-checking and rectification should prove easy. Indeed, many require only a degree of common sense. For example, anyone should be able to use a depth gauge to assess the depth amount of tread on a tyre, and ascertaining whether the front and rear lights are operative is the work of less than a minute for the driver and a helper.

Let's face it, failing the MoT test is bad enough, but failing for something trivial just adds insult to the extra cost of the re-test!

❏ TIME SCALE

There's a year between tests, so they don't exactly come out of the blue. Around a month before the test is due (stick the date in your diary) is the time to start checking over the obvious points. Why? Well, you can put your car in for its test a full calendar month in advance of the date on the certificate. This means that there is plenty of time to correct any major problems that occur. Moreover, it means that you get a 13 month certificate if you pass!

Take your car in 'on spec' without having given it a once-over and the odds are stacked against the car getting through. Even if you have your car regularly serviced, you really do need to give it a thorough check before the test - unless, of course, you take it in for a pre-MoT examination beforehand.

❏ GREY AREAS

It's generally acknowledged within the trade (and without it for that matter) that the present MoT test has within it some very grey areas; places where the difference between a pass and a fail is very much down to the skill and opinion of the tester.

Most obvious is that of bodywork checks, an area introduced in 1993, the essence of which is that no part of the bodywork should constitute a danger to other road users. What constitutes a danger and what doesn't can often be open to interpretation.

Some things are clearly dangerous; for example, a missing bumper which leaves a rusty mounting bracket sticking out will attract pedestrians' shins like a magnet. But what if there is a rusty hole on top of the wing? A hole in the *side* of the wing could be dangerous because a jagged edge might snag a pedestrian, but a hole on top would *generally* not be thought to be so.

But, it is down to the opinion of the tester and he will, of course, judge it in the context of the condition of the rest of the car. Let's face it, a car with so much body rot is likely to be old and well-worn and it may be that the hole in question is likely to get much worse well before the next MoT. At the end of the day, it's the tester's job to ensure that the only cars running on Britain's roads are safe cars. There are other areas which don't stand up to close examination; for example, it is the law for post-1965 cars to have seat belts fitted (at least in the front) and these form part of the test. However, child seats are not tested, despite the fact that some DIY fitting thereof borders on the criminal!

❏ "FIRST USED" - A DEFINITION

In many of the chapters, you will come across the term 'first used' in conjunction with a date; for example, the minimum tyre tread depth of 1.6mm applies to all passenger cars first used after the 2nd January 1933.

For the purpose of the MoT test this means;

a) The date of manufacture if the vehicle has not been registered for use on the road (eg. imported cars or those used by the armed forces).

b) A date 6 months after the date of its manufacture OR the date it was first registered - whichever is the earlier.

❏ CLEANING UP

By the time you take your car for the test, you should be pretty confident it will pass. Nevertheless, it's a good idea to make sure that it's reasonably clean; you'll feel better and it could show up faults you hadn't seen before - a cracked headlamp lens, for example.

If you can, use a garage 'jet wash' and clear some of the caked on gunge from under the car; again, you might discover a potential failure point.

Whilst no tester is going to pass a vehicle with faults, no matter how clean, he will appreciate not getting covered in three months' worth of dirt and grime while he performs his duties. Indeed, if a car is dirty enough, a tester can actually refuse to test it!

The blue 'three triangles' symbol can only be displayed by garages who meet the standards set by the DoT. Note in this case that the garage can test diesel-engined cars - not all can.

❏ GETTING IN THE PICTURE

Where you are dismantling complex assemblies (a brake disc/calliper, for example), make sure that you know exactly what goes where and in what order. The old method of scribbling down rough diagrams still works, but you can use modern technology to make life easier. If you have a Polaroid camera, you can produce an exact, and instant, representation of what you're working on. Better yet, if you have a camcorder, you can (as we did) make it work for a living by setting it up on a tripod to film the whole dismantling procedure. This also allows you to add a 'commentary', noting any particular points you will need to remember when it comes to reassembly.

❏ WHERE TO START

Your car can only be tested at an approved MOT testing station - approved, that is, by the Department of Transport. Not all stations can test all types of vehicle - what they can should be clearly shown at their premises, along with various other vital (to the customer) pieces of information, such as the right to appeal, the current fees applicable and examiners' qualifications. The blue 'three triangles' symbol can only be displayed by garages who meet the standards set by the DoT.

❏ QUESTION TIME

The MoT test is shrouded in mystery, so here are the answers to some of the most common questions.

Q   WHEN DOES MY CAR NEED AN MOT TEST?

A   All cars (*i.e.* those in MoT test class IV) must pass an MoT test annually, starting when (or just before) the car is three years old. If you are unsure as to the exact

MOT TEST CLASSES

Vehicle	Testing class	Test first req'd (yrs)
Motor cycles (up to 200cc)	I	3
All Motor cycles	II	3
3-wheeled cars up to 450 kgs (unladen)	III	3
Cars, goods vehicles up to 3000 kgs gross weight. Minibuses with up to 8 passenger seats. Minibuses with between 9 - 12 passenger seats. Motor caravans and dual purpose vehicles. Taxis and ambulances with up to 12 passenger seats.	IV	3
Private passenger vehicles and ambulances with more than 12 passenger seats	V	1
Public service vehicles*	VI	1
Goods vehicles between 3000 - 3500 kgs gross weight.	VII	3

PSVs MUST BE TESTED BY THE DEPARTMENT OF TRANSPORT.

'class' of your car, see the table in this chapter.

Q   WHO CAN TEST MY CAR?

A   Garages who employ qualified testers will have the '3 triangles' sign outside. However, not all garages are able to test all vehicles, particularly when it comes to commercial vehicles. With the 1993 controversy over diesel engines (resulting in a rule change for 1994), some garages opted out of testing cars so-powered. So, make it quite clear before you take your car for test *exactly* the type of vehicle you have.

Q   CAN A QUALIFIED GARAGE REFUSE TO TEST MY CAR?

A   If you present your car for a pre-booked test, the garage must test it. However, there are certain caveats, and the garage can legally refuse to test your car if:

a) It is so dirty the test is practically impossible.

b) It has an insecure load or is too large/heavy for the capabilities of the testing equipment.

c) The registration document is required and it is not available.

d) The vehicle is incapable of being driven.

e) Having started a test, the tester has the right to stop testing if he considers the vehicle to be unsafe in any way, for example, if the driver's seat mountings are corroded and it is considered dangerous to perform the braking test.

Q   CAN I TAKE MY CAR FOR A TEST BEFORE THE DATE ON THE PREVIOUS CERTIFICATE?

A   Yes, see below.

Q   IF I HAVE MY CAR SUCCESSFULLY TESTED BEFORE THE EXPIRY DATE OF MY EXISTING MOT CERTIFICATE, DO I 'LOSE' THAT TIME?

A   Not necessarily. In fact, many people take their cars in early for the test to allow some leeway for any repairs that may be required. As long as the original certificate expiry date is less than a calendar month away, the new certificate can be forward-dated to ensure that no days are lost - in fact, it can actually mean that you get a 13 month MOT!

Q   WHAT IS THE PASS CERTIFICATE?

A   Officially, it is form VT20, issued by authorised garages. It records the following details about your car:

The registration mark.

Chassis number.

Colour.

Year of manufacture.

The engine capacity.

The fuel type.

The mileage.

It also shows the date tested (and date of expiry of a previous certificate where applicable) and the signature of the tester. It must be embossed with the details of the testing garage - see below.

The details of the testing garage must be *embossed* (it is not sufficient for the garage ink stamp to be applied) on the lower part of both pass *and* failure certificates using the special machine supplied. It is important to check that your certificate has been fully and correctly completed, otherwise it could be deemed illegal.

Q   WHAT ABOUT FORGED MOT CERTIFICATES?

A   There are some very good forged MOT certificates around and so it pays to take care when you're buying a used car with, ap-

The Department of Transport

Test Certificate

Serial number

The motor vehicle of which the Registration Mark

G 836 VYV

PD 0106853

having been examined under section 45 of the Road Traffic Act 1988, it is hereby certified that at the date of the examination thereof the statutory requirements prescribed by Regulations made under the said section 45 were complied with in relation to the vehicle.

Vehicle identification or chassis number — *JM ZMA18B 200 ⌷⌷⌷*

Vehicle Testing Station Number — *78083*

Vehicle category — *TED*

Date of issue — *DECEMBER 13ᵗʰ 1993 (NINTHREE)*

Make — *MAZDA*

Date of first use — *1989*

Date of expiry — *DECEMBER 12ᵗʰ 19... (NINTH...*

Recorded mileage — *27319*

If a goods vehicle, maximum design gross weight — *N/A* kg

Serial Number of immediately preceding Test Certificate

(To be entered when above date of expiry is more than ... after the above date of issue)

If not a goods vehicle, horse power or cylinder capacity of engine in cubic centimetres — *1600 cc*

Fuel type — *PETROL*

Signature of tester/inspector — *S. Rob*

Name in BLOCK CAPITALS — *S. BRANT*

Authentication Stamp

WARNING

A Test Certificate should not be accepted as evidence of the satisfactory mechanical condition of a used vehicle offered for sale.

CHECK

carefully that the particulars quoted above are correct. Certificates showing alterations should not be issued or accepted. They may delay the renewal of a Licence.

VT20

10

Embossing MoT Failure Certificate.

parently, a long MoT. To date, the watermark in the paper cannot be reproduced - check it before you buy.

Q   MUST I TAKE MY PREVIOUS CERTIFICATE?

A   You should do. This means that the tester can date it 364 days from its date. Keeping hold of consecutive test certificates is also a very good way of validating mileage claims when you come to sell your car. However, if you do not have your previous test certificate, the tester will make out a new one

dated the actual date of the test.

Q   WHAT HAPPENS IF I CAN'T FIND MY TEST CERTIFICATE AT RENEWAL TIME?

A   As mentioned above, you don't actually need it to renew your MOT test, even though you may lose a week or two's 'grace.'

Q   I HAVE AN MOT CERTIFICATE; THEREFORE MY CAR IS ROAD LEGAL, ISN'T IT?

A   Not necessarily. For cars over 3 years old it is a legal requirement to have a valid MOT certificate, but your car could actually become *illegal* a mile down the road from the testing station; for example, a brake light bulb could fail. It follows that maintaining your car in a truly legal state is an ongoing process and the responsibility of the car owner. There are various notices that MoT testing stations are required to show - the one illustrated makes it quite clear that it's up to you to ensure that your car is roadworthy *at all times*, not just on the day of the test.

Q   WHAT HAPPENS IF I AM STOPPED

Note this warning.

Left: MoT Pass Certificate (Form VT20).
(Crown Copyright Reserved. Reproduced with the permission of the Controller of Her Majesty's Stationery Office).

Road Traffic Act 1988 sections 45 and 46

Customer's Copy

Notification of a Refusal to issue an MOT Test Certificate
(IMPORTANT: Read notes overleaf)

Serial No. 82863365 AA

● Please keep this copy as your record of the test failure.

Vehicle Reg. Mark:	TSU 969	Make & Model:	DODGE 6250cc	Weight:		Year of Manufacture 1959	Class of Vehicle
VIN or Chassis No.:	AOL 00169 4	Recorded Mileage:	74734		Colour:	PINK	I II III IV V VII

A Items tested.	Manual ref.		Pass	Fail	Reasons for failure
Lighting Equipment	Cars & LGV	Motor cycles			
Front & rear lamps	I/1		✓		
Headlamps	I/2		✓		
Headlamp aim	I/6		✓		
Stop lamps	I/3		✓		
Rear reflectors	I/4		✓		
Direction indicators	I/5		✓		
Steering and Suspension	Cars & LGV	Motor cycles			*front tie bar bush worn out.*
Steering control	II/1	II/1	✓		
Steering mechanism/system	II/2	II/2	✓		
Power steering	II/3	N/A	N/A		
Transmission shafts	II/2,4,9	N/A	N/A		
Wheel bearings	II/4	II/3,4			
Front suspension	II/5-9	II/3	R	✓	
Rear suspension	II/9	II/4	✓		
Shock absorbers	II/10	II/3,4	✓		
Wheel alignment	N/A	II/5	✓		
Brakes	Cars & LGV	Motor cycles			
Controls and A.B.S. warning system	III/1,3	III/1	N/A		
Condition of service brake system	III/3,4	III/2	✓		
Condition of parking brake system	III/1,2	N/A	✓		
Service brake performance	III/5-8	III/3			
Parking brake performance	III/5-8	N/A			
Tyres and Wheels	Cars & LGV	Motor cycles			
Tyre type	IV				
Tyre load/speed rating (Class VII)			N/A		
Tyre condition			✓		
Roadwheels			✓		
Seatbelts	Cars & LGV				
Mountings					
Condition		N/A	N/A		
Operation		N/A			
Motor Cycle Side Car	Cars & LGV	Motor cycles			
Security	N/A	V/1			
Suspension / wheel	N/A	V/2	N/A		
Wheel align	N/A	V/3			
General	Cars & LGV	Motor cycles			*screen washer not working*
Windscreen wipers &	VI/1,2		R	✓	
Horn	VI/4	VI/1	✓		
Exhaust system	VI/3	VI/2	✓		
Exhaust emissions		N/A	✓		
Vehicle structure	VI/5	VI/3	✓		
Speed limiter (Class V)			N/A		

B I Certify that for the reasons shown above the vehicle has failed to comply with the statutory requirements

Authentication Stamp

Signed: (Tester/Inspector) *G. Moorcroft* Date: 23/6/92

Name: (in CAPITALS) G. MOORCROFT Testing Station No.: 78083

C Warning: In my opinion, the vehicle is dangerous to drive because of the following defects*

*delete if not appropriate

VT30 (Rev. Aug. 1991)

MoT Failure Certificate (Form VT30). (Crown Copyright Reserved. Reproduced with the permission of the Controller of Her Majesty's Stationery Office).

12

MOT INSPECTION CHECK LIST

THIS FORM MUST NOT BE USED AS AN MOT FAILURE DOCUMENT.

IT IS **ONLY** TO BE USED AS A CHECK LIST OF TESTABLE ITEMS AND FOR ADVISING CUSTOMERS OF COMPONENTS, WHETHER TESTABLE OR NOT, WHICH ARE OR MAY BECOME DEFECTIVE BEFORE THE NEXT MOT OR SERVICE IS DUE.

IF THE VEHICLE FAILS THE TEST A VT30 MUST BE ISSUED.

| Vehicle Reg. Mark | Make & Model: | | CC: | | Year of Manufacture: |
| VIN or Chassis No.: | Recorded Mileage: | | Colour: | | Weight: |

A Items tested.	Manual ref.			Pass	Fail	DEFECTS/COMMENTS
Lighting Equipment	Class V	Cars & LGV	Motor Cycles			
Front & rear lamps etc	I/1,6,8	1.1	I/1			
Headlamps	I/2	1.2	I/2			
Headlamp aim	I/9	1.6	I/6			
Stop lamps	I/3	1.3	I/3			
Rear reflectors	I/4	1.4	I/4			
Direction indicators & hazard lamps	I/5,7	1.5	I/5			
Steering and Suspension	Class V	Cars & LGV	Motor Cycles			
Steering control	II/1	2.1	II/1			
Steering mechanism/system	II/2	2.2	II/2			
Power steering	II/3	2.3	N/A			
Transmission shafts	II/5	2.5	N/A			
Wheel bearings	II/5	2.5	II/3,4			
Front suspension	II/4,5	2.4,5	II/3			
Rear suspension	II/4	2.4,6	II/4			
Shock absorbers	II/6	2.7	II/3,4			
Wheel alignment	N/A	N/A	II/5			
Brakes	Class V	Cars & LGV	Motor Cycles			
ABS warning system/controls	N/A	3.4	III/1			
Condition of service brake system	III/3,5	3.3,5,6	III/2			
Condition of parking brake system	III/1,2,4	3.1,2,5	N/A			
Service brake performance	III/7	3.7	III/			
Parking brake performance	III/7	3.7	N/			
Additional braking devices	III/6	N/A	N/A			
Tyres and Wheels	Class V		Motor Cycles			
Tyre type	IV/1					
Tyre load/speed ratings (Class V & VII)	IV/1					
Tyre condition	IV/1		IV/1			
Roadwheels						
Seatbelts		Cars & LGV				
Mountings/Condition/Operation		5.1	N/A			
Motor Cycle Sidecar		Cars & LGV	Motor Cycles			
Security		N/A	V/1			
Suspension & wheel bearings		N/A	V/2			
Wheel alignment		N/A	V/3			
General	Class V	Cars & LGV	Motor Cycles			
Drivers view of the road	VI/4,15	6.1	N/A			
Horn	VI/5	6.2	VI/1			
Exhaust system	VI/8	6.3	VI/2			
Exhaust emissions	VI/10	6.4	N/A			
General vehicle condition	VI/1, 2, 11,12,13, 14,16,17	6.5	VI/3			
Mirrors	VI/3	6.6	N/A			
Fuel system	VI/9	6.7	N/A			
Registration plates and VIN numbers	N/A	6.8	N/A			
Speedo	VI/6	N/A	N/A			
Speed limiter	VI/7	N/A	N/A			

GARAGE STAMP

| Signed: (Tester/Inspector) | Date: |
| Name: (in Capitals) | Testing Station No.: |

Cdf 104376/2/0229368 12m pads 3/93 DTP

Inspection checklist. (Crown Copyright Reserved. Reproduced with the permission of the Controller of Her Majesty's Stationery Office).

BY THE POLICE AND ASKED FOR MY MOT CERTIFICATE BUT HAVEN'T GOT IT IN THE CAR?

A You will be allowed a maximum of seven days to produce it at a police station.

Q WHAT HAPPENS IF THE POLICE WANT TO SEE MY CERTIFICATE BUT I CAN'T FIND IT?

A You can obtain a duplicate certificate from either the issuing test station or the DoT. If obtaining one is likely to take more than the original seven day period, you must tell the police what is happening.

Q WHAT HAPPENS IF MY CAR *FAILS* THE TEST?

A You will be issued with a form VT30 which will list details of all items which have contributed to the test failure. Previously, this would also show items which the tester believed would soon be creating problems, though this has now been changed. This form should not be confused with the MOT inspection check list which is for use only to advise customers of components whether testable or not which are, or are likely to become, defective before the next MOT or service is due.

Q WHAT DO I HAVE TO PAY?

A If you leave your car at the testing station for the necessary repair work to be carried out, there will be no re-test fee. If you take your car away, then the full re-test fee will usually be payable (see next question). Take into account that, from time to time, garages run special proMOTions with regard to test/re-test fees. At the time of writing, one local garage was giving away Marks & Spencer vouchers with every MOT issued!

Q WHEN I TAKE MY CAR FOR A RE-TEST, WHAT IS TESTED?

A Not just the failure points, as many people think. A re-test is just that - a complete MOT test of all the points normally checked. However, there are certain exceptions; if your car fails with faults relating to any of the following items and you take it back (*rectified*) prior to the end of the next *working* day, then just those items will be re-tested and there will be no extra fee - Seatbelts (but not the anchorages), doors (including boot/hatch), number plates, VIN plate, headlamp aim, front/rear position lamps and reflectors, indicators (including hazard lamps), exhaust emissions, windscreen (and washers/ wipers), mirrors and horn.

Q WHAT HAPPENS IF I DISAGREE WITH THE TESTER'S OPINION?

A Firstly, make your disagreement known to the tester - in a reasonable manner. If you believe your car is subject to special exemptions (older cars, for example, often have to comply to different, usually less stringent, rules) then you should have some way of backing up your claim. If you simply disagree, and neither he, nor the garage owner will see your point of view, you have the right of appeal to the vehicle inspectorate - the garage will supply the form required to lodge your appeal, reference number VT17. You have fourteen days to appeal after which the inspectorate will consider the merits of your case. When the car is re-tested, you will have to pay for it, whether it passes or not.

The 'red-tape' involved is more than a little and, of course, you must not have any repairs done in the meantime. Unless you feel *really* strongly about a particular point, it's probably simpler (and cheaper in the long run) to take your car to another testing station and see what they say.

Q   WHAT ABOUT THE LEGALITY OF DRIVING AFTER MY CAR HAS FAILED THE TEST?

A   Once your car has failed a test, the official ruling is that you can only drive it in order to get to and from the testing station and on a journey specifically connected with effecting repairs. More importantly, you **MUST** make a specific appointment before starting your journey - it's not enough to argue that you were on your way to the garage on the off-chance they could re-test your car. If, because of a lack of MOT certificate, your car has no tax, then it is permissible to drive to and from a pre-booked MOT test appointment. You should bear in mind that you may not be insured if your car is on a public road without an MOT certificate. It's best to check before - not after - the event. Despite the official line, you could still be prosecuted and/or fined for driving a vehicle in an unroadworthy condition in certain circumstances - where your car has a major brake fault, or tyres in a dangerous condition, for example.

Q   WHAT HAPPENS IF I AM CAUGHT DRIVING MY CAR WITHOUT A CURRENT MOT CERTIFICATE?

A   The current maximum fine is £1000!

SAFETY HINTS & TOOLS

❏ SAFETY

Many checks and rectification procedures can be carried out by anyone with reasonable DIY ability. Saving money is a good reason for carrying out any preparation/rectification work yourself, as long as it doesn't cost you dear in other ways. Whenever you are working on your car, personal safety, and that of anyone else involved, must be uppermost in your mind. By definition, a motor car is an inherently dangerous beast, even when it's stationary; there are around twenty UK fatalities every year involving jacks, ramps or axle stands - the 'injuries' list is much longer, featuring such horrors as burns, bruises, asphyxia, fractures and crushing. It's not difficult to ensure that your name does not appear

Disconnect the earth terminal first.

on someone's list of 'horror' statistics. Follow these simple tips and apply common sense and you'll make your motoring life easier, safer and a lot less painful.

When you're working on your electrical or fuel system, it's always wise to disconnect the earth (usually negative/-) terminal of the battery. Your car's handbook will tell you whether it's positive or negative earth. If you have a battery back-up alarm you'll have to switch it to 'valet' mode first and if you've a coded radio/cassette deck, make sure you know what the code is! If you have a sealed-for-life battery, read the specific instructions with regard to its treatment, charging etc. Remember that battery acid is particularly nasty stuff, so keep it away from your skin and the vehicle bodywork. Like petrol, it gives off harmful and explosive vapours.

It is, thankfully, becoming ever more common to find motorists with fire extinguishers fitted in the car, the garage or both. Whenever you are working on your car, make sure that yours is to hand - and that you know how to use it! This applies particularly when you are working on your car's fuel system.

If you need to raise the car (and many pre MoT checks can only be done with the car off the ground) you must be extremely careful. Work on level, firm ground and,

A trolley jack is best if you need to raise the car.

you only get one pair! When you're working under the car, there's the constant likelihood that there will be bits of dirt and maybe even rust falling around you. If you don't wear goggles, you could seriously damage your eyesight. Even if, like me, you wear glasses, there are goggles designed just for us, so that you can protect your eyes *and* still be able to see straight! You should also wear eye protection when using machinery (electric drills, sanders, grinders, etc) likely to produce

ideally, use a suitable trolley jack to raise the car; at a push, use the vehicle's wheel-changing jack, but remember that it will be nowhere near as capable as a trolley jack because it was designed for emergencies only and not for supporting the weight of the car for long periods of time.

NEVER, EVER get underneath a car supported **only** by a jack of any description. If the job permits, use ramps to raise the front or rear of the car. If ramps are not practicable, use axle stands to take the weight over a period of time. Unless the job you are doing necessitates otherwise, leave the handbrake on and the car in a low gear or "Park". **ALWAYS chock the wheels still on the ground.**

Protect your eyes -

Always ensure the car is safely supported before getting underneath it.

airborne detritus. It's also a good idea to wear strong gloves to protect your hands, particularly if your car is of the age where there is likely to be plenty of rusted metal with sharp edges around. Gardening gloves are OK for general inspection work and cleaning.

SAFETY HINTS AND TIPS

• *Whenever you are working on your car, remove the ignition key. If power is required for a specific check (headlamps, for example) then take great care that it is not accidentally left on, and put the car neutral, in case the key is accidentally turned from the 'on' position to the 'start' position.*

• *Get into the habit of coating your hands with barrier cream before you start any dirty work. It makes them easier to clean when you finish and helps offset the detrimental affects of oil and grease on the skin.*

• *Do not allow children to play in or around a car you are working on.*

• *Do not smoke (or allow others to) when you are working on your car.*

• *If you need to check items beneath the car (exhaust, suspension etc.) make sure that it cannot move; put the car in a low gear and put the handbrake on. As a 'belt and braces' measure chock the front and rear wheels.*

• *Whenever you are working on your car, and particularly if you are working under it, it's a good idea to have a helper on hand - even if it's only for moral support. Failing that, make sure that someone knows where you are and checks on you occasionally.*

• *If you need your engine to be running for a specific check, **NEVER** do so in the confines of your garage: always work outdoors. Exhaust fumes can kill within minutes - even if they've been passed through a catalytic converter.*

• *Keep your car's vital fluids away from your skin wherever possible. Oil, anti-freeze, petrol, diesel and brake/power steering fluid etc will do you a power of no good.*

• *On the same subject, any spillage should be wiped up straight away. Where the floor is likely to remain slippery, use granules (cat litter does the same job) to soak up the excess.*

• *If you're working in the engine bay, do so with a cool (preferably cold) engine. Remember that many modern cars have electric cooling fans which switch on thermostatically several minutes after the engine has been switched off.*

• *If you need the engine to be running for a specific check, take great care not to get caught up in the moving parts (drivebelts etc.). Don't wear any loose clothing and keep your long hair under your cap. Remember that the voltage from electronic ignition systems can be tens of thousands of volts! Remove watches, rings or other jewellery which could get in the way or cause an electrical short.*

• If a job needs two people, use two people - struggling on your own is a recipe for disaster.

• If you have a first aid kit (an excellent addition for any car) keep it open on the bench in case you need it quickly.

• Keep a supply of water handy in case you get any corrosive substances on your skin - battery acid for example.

• One of the easiest ways to hurt yourself is to use the wrong tool for the job. Don't do it!

• Be careful not to breathe in dangerous fumes.

• When using 240v power tools, take great care with the mains lead, especially if you need to use an extension cord. Make sure that no-one can trip over it and that it cannot be trapped or damaged.

❏ TOOLS REQUIRED

In general, few special tools are required to rectify typical pre-MoT problems. The advice is, as always, to make sure that the tools you use are of good quality and not likely to let you down in your hour of need. Buy from a respected manufacturer and get a good warranty.

A good socket set is the bedrock of the DIY motorist's tool set. Make sure that you've got a good selection of suitable sockets (most modern cars use metric nuts and bolts). By-and-large, if you can get a socket to the fastener in question, then that's the tool you should use. However, if you can't, you'll have

to use a spanner (or on occasion, an adjustable wrench). Buying a set of combination spanners, where one end is an open end and the other is a ring, is a good way to start your collection.

A set of screwdrivers is also a good investment. By having a selection ranging from a small electrical version up to a 300mm/12inch bruiser, you'll never have any excuse for using the wrong 'driver for an application - something that can sometimes result in a damaged fastener, car or person!

When you're repairing part of your car that can be removed, a stable workplace is essential. Ideally, you'll have a sturdy workbench, like the Warco model which features a lockable cabinet, ideal for storing the dangerous products associated with DIY motoring (brake cleaner, heavy duty adhesives etc).

The Black & Decker Workmate makes an excellent mobile substitute and is particularly useful for those with only small garages or who have to work totally *al fresco*.

The most useful power tool you can have is, of course, an electric drill. It's a versatile machine which can be used in many ways in addition to its obvious original purpose of drilling holes. For MoT purposes, one of the most productive ways it can be put to work is by fitting a wire brush and discovering what's beneath all that mud and dirt under your car.

Cordless drills have become very much part of the DIY motoring scene, and with good reason. There's plenty of power available for all but the most arduous of tasks,

Cordless version of the ever-useful electric drill.

1kg and 2kg fire extinguishers, suitable for car and garage.

and the smaller size and lack of cable makes them far easier to use. Make sure you use the right machine for the job in hand; a heavy de-rusting job, for example, requires mains power.

LIGHTING

❏ OVERVIEW

LENSES

All lamps must be secure and lenses should be clean and free from serious damage - for example, a slight crack in a rear lamp lens would probably not be too much cause for concern, as long as the security of its mounting was not affected nor the intensity of the light. However, if the lens had been smashed and white light was showing through, this would not be acceptable. Repairs to a lens *are* acceptable as long as the lamp emits sufficient light of the correct colour and is secure. All lamps must be securely mounted on the vehicle.

NOT FADE AWAY

With the obvious exception of the indicators, all lamps should show a steady light and not fade or flicker when tapped lightly. If they flicker, the most likely cause is that the terminals inside are loose or corroded or that there is an earthing problem somewhere. These faults occur more frequently in direct relation to the age of the car.

It is usually a simple task to get access to the bulb and its connections, either by removing the outer lens or by unclipping the inner circuit board. Remove the offending bulb and check the connections for security. Application of emery paper to the various metal connectors and the metal parts of the bulb will usually produce a good result. Whilst you're in there, it's a good idea to give the other bulbs and connectors the same treatment.

THE KNOCK-ON EFFECT

The tester will also check that operation of one set of lights does not affect the operation of another. For example, it is not uncommon for the application of the brake lamps to dim the position (side) lamps. In extreme circumstances, there are cases where, for example, operating the indicator switch causes the brake light to flash when the brakes are applied at the same time! This type of fault can (again) usually be traced to bad earthing at some point. Start at the offending bulb(s) and work back down the line, systematically cleaning all the connections and making sure that any earth terminal is making good solid contact with clean metal. With older cars, the earth terminals are often connecting with 80% rust!

No light? Most modern cars have plug-in lamp clusters like the one illustrated, where it's easy to use a tester to check whether voltage is reaching the bulb. If it is then either the bulb itself has failed (you'll probably be able to see a broken filament) or even more common is a poor earth. The latter is usually caused by a build-up of corrosion.

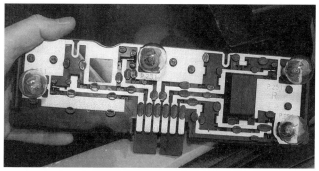

warning.

When everything appears to be working inside the car, it's time to enlist the help of an assistant to check that the lights are doing what they should be.

Application of a little time and emery paper will usually do the trick.

REVERSING LAMPS
As yet, reversing lamps do not form part of the MoT test.

SYMMETRY
The tester will not make an accurate check as to the position of headlamps or front and rear position lamps, indicator lamps or brake lamps. However, they should all be visually symmetrical, ie, positioned the same distance inboard from the edges of the car and at the same height.

SWITCH OPERATION
The most logical place to start is inside the car where you can check that the following lighting switchgear is securely mounted and works correctly;

Side/main beam/dip beam

Indicators (including hazard lights)

Rear fog lamp

Visual tell-tale indicators are required for the main headlamp beam, the rear fog lamps and the indicators. In addition, the indicators must also have an *audible*

❏ FRONT AND REAR POSITION LAMPS (SIDE LIGHTS)
'Position lamp' is the official term for what most people call the side light. All cars have to have front and rear position lamps, headlamps and brake lamps. There are some exceptions, but these are fairly obscure and not likely to be of interest or relevance to the average motorist.

At the front, the position lamps must show a steady white light, though where they are part of a headlamp assembly which emits a yellow light, that colour is also permissible.

At the rear, there should be two lamps emitting a steady red light and, like the front lamps, they should be visible from a 'reasonable' distance. Any position lamps other than these four are, by definition, optional and not subject to the lamp testing procedure (though their security of mounting may be). At least 50% of the lamps must be visible from the front or rear as applicable.

❑ HEADLAMPS AND FRONT DRIVING FOG LAMPS

The tester will check to ensure that the vehicle is fitted with a matched pair of main beam/dipped beam headlamps. The lamps should be a matched pair of the same size.

There are three different types of headlamp and so you must check which is yours before you start adjusting. Most common is the European style, which can be recognised by the 'stepped' pattern in the headlamp glass. These are checked on dipped beam.

The other two types are both called British American, but some are checked on dipped beam and some on full beam. BA lamps marked with a figure '2' or '2a' must be checked on dipped beam whereas those marked '1' or '1a'

The headlamp beam aim will be checked by the tester on sophisticated and accurate equipment, not available to the average motorist.

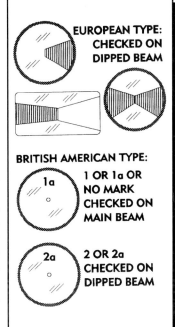

EUROPEAN TYPE: CHECKED ON DIPPED BEAM

BRITISH AMERICAN TYPE:

1a — 1 OR 1a OR NO MARK CHECKED ON MAIN BEAM

2a — 2 OR 2a CHECKED ON DIPPED BEAM

The three different types of headlamp are illustrated here.

(or with no marking at all), are checked on full beam.

FOUR-HEADLAMP SYSTEMS

In a 4-headlamp system, it is not a requirement for the outer pair to emit the same colour light as the inner pair. However, the outer pair is required to provide the *dipped* beam. Because of the wording of the test (in that only the *obligatory* lamps are checked) inner lamps which provide a main beam only are not checked.

FRONT DRIVING OR FOGLAMPS

Likewise, because front fog and spot (or driving) lamps are not 'ob-

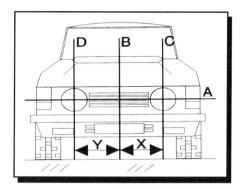

ligatory' they do not form part of the test, other than to check that they a securely mounted and are unlikely to cause harm to another road user.

DIY BEAM SETTING

By definition, home testing of head-lamp beam alignment has to be fairly simplistic, but by using the good old 'garage door' method and some care, you can usually achieve a good result. It won't be as accurate as the official tester, but if you can get near enough, it may be just a turn of an adjuster to bring them right into line.

Firstly, you need to locate your headlamp beam adjusters. These usually take the form of screw-adjusters, one on each lamp for up/down and side/side adjustment. On older cars, removal of chrome trim may be necessary.

Even if you're not going to adjust the headlamps your-self, you should make sure that they are fully operative and that the adjusters are not rusted solid; a friendly tester will probably be quite happy to adjust your lights by a turn or two, rather than issue a failure certificate, but he won't want to get involved in freeing-off rust-seized screw

threads! Apply a little grease to the threads to smooth their way.

Perform the test with the car on level ground approximately 6-7ft away from any vertical surface - your garage door is ideal.

As you need to see where your headlamp beams are aimed, you won't be able to work properly in bright sunlight; work in a shaded area or during darkness.

Take a tape measure and measure the distance from the ground

... and transfer them to a vertical surface (e.g. garage door).

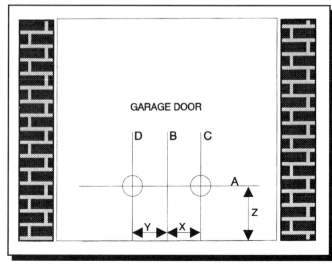

to the centre of the headlamps. Transfer that reading to the wall/door and make a horizontal chalk mark (A). Then draw a vertical line at a position corresponding with the centre of the car (B). Add two more vertical lines (C & D) to bisect line (A) where the centre of the headlamps would be. The distances X & Y must be the same.

During the test, it is important that your car should be square to the door or wall at its natural attitude, *i.e.* not weighed down with your holiday luggage. The most natural load for the average owner is with a half tank of fuel and just the driver. This is handy, as it means your helper, required to switch the lights on and off, can sit in the driver's seat.

The first check is to ensure that the lights work (side/head/dip) and that when switched to dip, they go down toward the left. Most lamps should be adjusted whilst on dipped beam so they can be set not to dazzle oncoming drivers whilst, at the same time, maximize the available light for the driver.

Cover one of the lights and switch the headlamps to dip setting. When you look at the beam on the vertical surface, you'll see a patch of light which is particularly bright - this is the 'hot spot.' For the most popular type of lens (the European) this should be below the horizontal line and slightly to the left of the vertical line - the accompanying diagram makes this clearer.

HEADLAMP CONDITION
When checking your headlamps, you must make sure that the lamps

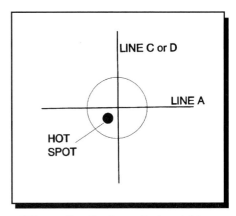

Where the 'hot spot' should be.

are secured firmly - use firm hand pressure to make sure that the mountings are not loose or rusty. (Some lamps use spring-loaded mountings - the inherent 'give' in these will not be a cause for a 'fail'. Look especially for cracks, often caused by stone chips. These are not necessarily reasons for failure, but such cracks can let in water and/or cause condensation within the lamp. Naturally, correct (matched) wattage bulbs should be fitted and working.

Condensation can build up and

Condensation build-up inside a lamp.

cause the beam pattern to be altered so that it is illegal and fails the test. Even if the initial effect is not enough to cause a test failure, the long term result will be that the reflector surface of the headlamp will corrode and, again, the beam pattern will be adversely affected. Depending on your car, replacement will involve purchasing a whole sealed beam unit or just the damaged item. It is possible to buy lamps from breakers' yards, though you should make a thorough check that you are not buying another lamp with exactly the same faults.

One way to prevent cracked and smashed headlamps (all too frequent on today's roads) is to fit a protective plastic covering over the lens. Companies such as Signam produce a range of made-to-fit covers and Metro Products market a kit whereby you can cut your own covers to suit whichever shape lamps you need. Whichever, they are considerably cheaper than new lenses or failing the MoT test.

EXCEPTION TO THE RULE
Headlamps are not required on vehicles first used before 1st January 1931. If such a vehicle is fitted with one or two optional headlamps, then there are specific rules with regard to the dip and main beam arrangements: Where one lamp is fitted, it must have a dip beam capability. Where there are two fitted, either both must dip or at least one should dip and the other extinguish altogether.

FOREIGN VEHICLES
An increasing number of LHD vehicles are being imported for permanent use in the UK and many of them retain the original head/dip beam arrangement which is, of course, designed for a right-hand dip pattern. There are proprietary kits for masking the lamps or modifying the beams and these are fine as long as the lamps meet the other criteria (detailed earlier) and that the kits are securely fixed.

❏ DIRECTION INDICATORS AND HAZARD WARNING LIGHTS
These are required on all vehicles used after 1st January 1936 and can take the form of two flashing lights at front and rear or a semaphore indicator on each side of the car. The indicators should give an amber light, unless the vehicle was first used before 1st September 1965, where it is permissible for both front indicators to be white and both rear indicators to be red (they may be combined with stop lamps or with side/rear lamps).

Naturally, the indicators should work as intended, e.g. when the tester selects right indication, the right side front/rear right indicators should operate. The flashing rate should be between 60 and 120 times per minute. If the flashing rate is particularly slow, try again with the engine running. If this improves the rate to an acceptable level, this will be sufficient for a tester. Where running the engine has no effect, there could be one or more poor earth connections or, alternatively, it could be that the indicator relay itself giving up the ghost - not usually a repairable item.

In general, relays of this type are

simple plug-in items in the car's fusebox and are designed to be fitted one way only.

If the audible/visual indicator flashes at a noticeably increased rate to usual, it often means that one of the indicators in the circuit is not functioning. This could be the fault of a blown bulb or, more likely, a corroded terminal causing intermittent contact. Replace the bulb, check connectors or clean earth terminals as required.

Where the indicators are of the bulb/lens type - as opposed to semaphore indicators - there should be two lenses at the front and two at the rear.

SIDE REPEATER INDICATOR LAMPS

The indicator lenses must be in good condition and, if they are coloured, not show any white light. Damaged lenses such as that shown here, are not necessarily failure points; it may be that the damage does not permit white light to show or that it is easily (and effectively) repairable with suitably coloured tape. However, if the damage were sufficient to be of a danger to pedestrians, it may be failed under the 'bodywork security' section.

It's been a trend of recent years to fit clear lenses to indicators and use a coloured bulb. If, as in this case, the lens is missing but the bulb still operates, then it would not usually be a cause for a failure. However, it would also not be wise for an owner to drive the car like this, because of the obvious danger of the bulb being smashed.

On vehicles first used after 1st April 1986, a side repeater lamp

Damaged indicator lenses - a cause of failure?

should be fitted and must work in conjunction with the other lamps in the indicator circuit.

SEMAPHORE SIGNALS

Where the direction indicators are of the semaphore type, the testing procedure is slightly different in that an audible/visual interior warning system is not required *as long as*

Clear lenses and coloured bulbs is a recent trend.

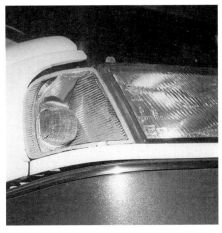

both semaphore arms can be seen from the drivers' seat. And, though the semaphore arm itself must illuminate in operation, it need not be a *flashing* light.

HAZARD WARNING LIGHTS
Hazard warning lights are required on all vehicles first used on or after 1st April 1986. However, if they are fitted to a vehicle, whatever the age, they will form part of the test. The tester will make sure that hazard lights work with the ignition on and off, that all the indicator lamps flash simultaneously and that the audible/visual warning device inside the car is working correctly.

❏ **STOP LAMPS**
Vehicles first used on or after 1st January 1971, must be fitted with two rear-facing stop lamps. A vehicle used before that date must feature at least one stop lamp, which should be fitted in line with the centre rear of the car, or towards the offside of it.

Where a vehicle has two lamps fitted (which in practical terms, is most cars on today's roads) it will

Additional stop lamp.

be treated as being in the first category, regardless of its age. Check that the lamp(s) operates when the foot brake is applied. At least 50% of the lamp must be visible from the rear.

Where additional stop lamps are fitted, whether by the manufacturer, as in the case of this Volvo pictured here, or by an individual owner, it must work in accordance with the rules for standard brakelights.

EXCEPTION TO THE RULE
Vehicles first used before 1st January 1936 are not required to be fitted with a stop lamp.

It is not a legal requirement to fit stop lamps where the vehicle is one of the few exceptions which does not require front or rear position lamps.

❏ **REAR REFLECTORS**
Each vehicle must carry two red reflectors on its rear, positioned symmetrically in horizontal and vertical planes. They should be clean and with plenty of reflective presence with at least 50% of the reflective surface visible from the rear.

Whilst the application of reflective tape to the rear of a car can

28

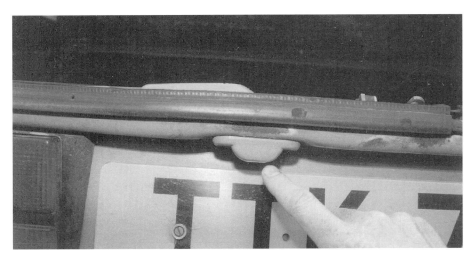

With the front and rear position lights (side lights) on, the rear registration light(s) must also illuminate.

be a genuine aid to night time visibility, it is *not* acceptable by an MoT tester as a substitute for a rear reflector. Most reflectors form an integral part of the rear stop/tail lamp lens assembly.

❏ REAR FOG LAMPS

Vehicles first used on or after 1st April 1980 are required to have at least one (fitted to the offside of the vehicle) rear fog lamp. This lamp or lamps should only operate with the ignition on and the front/rear position lamps illuminated. There must be an operational visual tell-tale light where the driver can

see it. This is often to be found in the switch itself.

❏ REAR REGISTRATION PLATE LAMPS

With the front and rear position lights (side lights) on, the rear registration light(s) must also illuminate. Where there is more than one bulb, they must all work - not doing so will mean test failure.

This is a fairly recent introduction to the MoT and many owners freely admit to never having noticed that their car has a registration plate light! It's easy to check and easy to replace bulbs if they've failed.

STEERING & SUSPENSION

❏ SAFETY

For most of the checks mentioned here, it will be necessary to get under the car and/or start the engine. Please refer to the safety section at the front of the book and always take extreme care when raising your car with a view to working underneath it. **NEVER** get beneath a car supported only by a jack - of **ANY** description. Protect your eyes and your hands when you are working under a car.

The areas of steering and suspension are ones where special tools are required in abundance and where trying to work without them can lead to serious problems. As with the braking system, if you have any doubt as to your ability to either judge the suitability of a particular component or to adjust/repair it, then take it to a specialist.

❏ A LITTLE KNOWLEDGE

There's a large variety of steering and suspension systems around and it's impossible to cover them all here. Make a date with your workshop manual and study the steering and suspension set-up of your own car so that you understand how it should work and know how to correct any faults you may find.

❏ CORROSION

There should be no serious corro-sion within 30cm (approx 12 inches) of any steering or suspension component or its mountings. This is covered in more detail later in the book, though corrosion is something you should always be on the lookout for.

❏ STEERING SYSTEMS

STEERING BOX

Most modern cars are fitted with a rack & pinion steering system (see below) the alternative being a steering box. Effectively, this is a small metal box containing various geared bevels which act to transfer the input from the steering column/wheel (via components such as the track rods) into the required movements of the steered wheels. Worn gears in the box often mean a replacement box is required, although many steering boxes are adjustable

RACK & PINION STEERING

This is the most common form of steering system found today. At the lower end of the steering shaft is a pinion which operates in a toothed section in the rack, a long piece of metal which runs from one side of the car to the other. The whole rack and pinion assembly must be fixed to the car in a secure manner.

Even this brief and simplistic explanation of steering basics makes it quite clear that there are a lot of

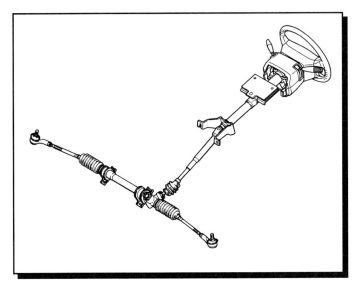

A typical rack and pinion and steering column assembly. (Courtesy Mazda)

- relative movement between a steering arm and its fixings.

When it comes to checking steering components under the front end of the car, the tester is looking basically joins and connections, all of which will wear, and offer the possibility for an MoT failure.

to see that everything is securely mounted to where it should be and that all components operate with the minimum of 'play.'

❏ EXCESSIVE WEAR

The essence of the test is that there should not be EXCESSIVE wear in the steering system. But what is excessive? In many cases, it will be patently obvious, but not so easy in others, which is where the skill and experience of the tester comes into play.

- insecurity of any part fixed to the vehicle structure (*e.g.* steering box, rack housing etc).
- relative movement between the sector shaft and the drop arm (steering box systems).
- a loose ball pin shank.
- a loose track rod or drag link end.
- a weak or broken socket spring.
- excessive play in a ball joint.
- excessive play in a pivot arm (*e.g.* an intermediate drop arm in steering box systems).

❏ POWER STEERING

Where a vehicle is fitted with power steering, the tester will run the engine when making his evaluation. The system should be free from leaks (which means all pipes and unions), though it will not fail just because of low steering fluid level.

Check your car's power steering by running the engine (outside - not in your garage) and having someone turn the steering wheel from side to side whilst you watch under the bonnet to ensure that fluid is not leaking whilst the system is in operation. If your fluid reservoir needs regular topping up, this points to a steady leak and one which should be found and sorted before the test.

Check the steering wheel to make sure that it is physically sound.

This is not likely to be a problem with modern, heavily padded wheels, but older cars with brittle plastic wheels may suffer from cracks and splits. It must, of course, be securely attached to the steering column shaft. Check also for excessive play in the column bearing, movement between the column shaft and steering wheel and security at the column top mounting bracket.

The steering column couplings/clamp bolts should be checked for security (by turning the wheel clockwise then anti-clockwise) and the steering wheel lock, where fitted, should be checked to ensure that it does lock the wheel when the ignition key is removed.

❏ CHECKING STEERING FREE PLAY

The steered wheels should be on the ground and, if power steering is fitted, the engine should be running. Take note of the safety rules at the start of the book.

With the road wheels pointing straight ahead, turn the steering wheel to the left and then to the right.

What you're looking for is for the road wheels to move as directly as possible with the movement of the steering wheel. The more

Steering rack gaiters, seen from under the car.

you can move the steering wheel before the wheels react ('free play'), the bigger the problem in the steering system and the greater the likelihood of a 'fail.' The tester will also make sure that on full lock, the steered wheels do not foul on anything under the car.

A failure certificate will be issued where the free play at the steering wheel is more than 13mm (approx 0.5 inch) for a car equipped with a rack and pinion* system and 75mm (approx 3 inches) for a non rack and pinion system.

These are quite hefty margins and if you're getting near these figures, you should investigate further. The rules assume a steering wheel of 380mm (approx 15 inch) diameter. Where the wheel is larger/smaller the free play limits will be raised/lowered accordingly.

Where there are several joints between the steering wheel and the rack, a movement of up to 48mm/approximately 1.9 inches (on a 380mm diameter steering wheel) may be acceptable.

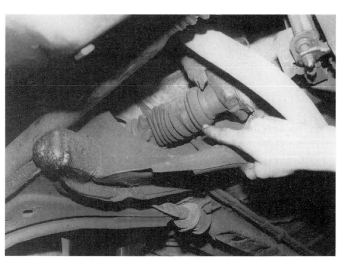

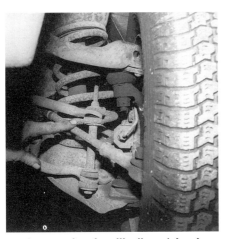

A worn bush will allow 'slop'.

Like the driveshaft gaiters (see later), these on the steering rack are there to prevent precious lubricating oil or grease getting out and dirt and dust getting in. They must be firmly attached and split-free.

On some cars, it's easier to see the gaiter from inside the engine bay. Don't forget to check the gaiters at both ends of the rack.

Rubber bushes are used exten-

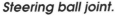

Steering ball joint.

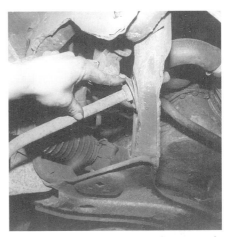

A failure point - and a danger - is this worn bush on a tie-rod.

sively in the steering and suspension systems and when you're checking your car, they are prime suspects. As you can see here, this particular bush has seen much better days and it would allow an enormous amount of 'slop.'

Where tie-rods bar are fitted, they should be mounted securely and show no appreciable play in

Anti-roll bar mounting secured by a castelated nut and split pin.

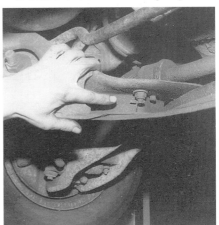

the mounting rubbers. The rubber bush on this one has worn to the point of disintegration. Apart from being a failure point, badly worn (or missing!) bushes make the car inherently dangerous to drive.

Excessive play at a ball joint is a common cause of MoT failure. Replacement is possible on a DIY basis, though a special balljoint splitter is required in most cases.

It doesn't have to be something big for your car to fail its MoT; here, an anti-roll bar mounting is secured by using a castelated nut and a split pin. If the latter is missing, it makes the car dangerous and a failure.

❏ SUSPENSION GENERAL

With all suspension systems, the tester will check that there is sufficient clearance between the axle or suspension and the chassis bump-stop and whether the suspension components are strong enough to hold the body away from the axles. Checks for corrosion will be made, as described in a later chapter.

❏ SUSPENSION CHECKING PROCEDURE

For vehicles with suspension - front or rear - as shown in Figure 1 (see suspension types diagram), the check will be for excessive vertical movement between the stub axles and axle beams although, technically, this would be better described as a steering wear fault. Figure 1 type suspension will also be subject to leaf spring checks as detailed later. Where the suspension is of the type shown in Figures 2 and 2A, the check is for vertical movement between swivel (kingpin) and housing and movement in wishbone bushes. For all three checks, the suspension must be jacked up.

For vehicles with suspension

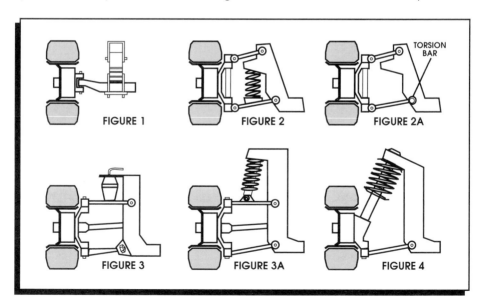

FIGURE 1 FIGURE 2 FIGURE 2A
FIGURE 3 FIGURE 3A FIGURE 4

types as shown in Figures 3, 3A and 4, the front wheels will be resting on turning plates, which enable the wheels to rotate lock to lock.

The tester will grasp the top of the front wheel and rock it to check for play in the upper and lower ball joints/wishbone bearing and the (Figure 4) MacPherson strut sliding bushes, glands and strut upper support bearings.

He will then change his grip on the wheel to 3 o'clock and 9 o'clock and shake the wheel to check the condition of the outer ball joints and the track control arm inner bushes.

Rear suspension systems will be similar to those front suspension systems illustrated, except, of course, there will be no swivel joints to allow for steering.

❏ **LEAF SPRINGS**
Leaf springs are becoming relatively rare on today's cars, but they're common for commercial vehicles and are still part of the test. The tester will first check that the springs are in good condition

Left: Common suspension systems. Although in each case front suspension systems are shown, generally rear suspension systems are similar. Figure 1: a leaf spring solid axle. Figure 2: wishbones and coil spring. Figure 2A: wishbones and torsional bar (the torsion bar runs longitudinally and is twisted by wishbone movement). Figure 3: wishbones and hydropneumatic sphere. Figure 3A: wishbones and coil spring. Figure 4: MacPherson strut.

The 'bounce' test for checking suspension.

(*i.e.* not cracked or fractured) and that they have not been damaged in any other way, for example, by a poor welded repair. Other failure points include -

- a defective spring eye.
- leaves so displaced that it impairs their operation and/or fouls on other parts of the car.
- a spring fitted so that the axle is misaligned.
- a shackle, anchor or linkage pin not correctly positioned or excessively loose in its bracket (or missing altogether).

The condition of the pins/bushes will be checked and excessive wear will result in a fail.

For example:
- 2mm wear for a 12mm diameter pin.
- 3mm wear for a 25mm diameter pin.
- 10% of the pin diameter for pins over 25mm diameter.

The MoT tester will want to raise the car in such a way as to take the strain off the suspension and associated components. This is usually achieved by using a jacking beam built into the vehicle lift: you can achieve the same effect with a jack and axle stands.

SHOCK ABSORBERS
The easiest check to perform on

suspension is the simple 'bounce' test - press down hard on the car and then release quickly. If the shock absorbers are in good order, the car will only take a couple of bounces to settle down. If it wallows around for a while, something is amiss and further investigation is required.

Telescopic shock absorbers are the norm nowadays (though there are still a few cars around featuring the earlier lever arm type, the MGB for example). It's vital that the dust shield at the top of telescopic shock absorbers is kept in place - this helps prevent dust and damaging grit getting in and ruining the seals and your chance of an MoT pass. Some shock absorbers will be fitted with rubber gaiters which should be in good condition for the same reason.

Check shock absorbers for security, in that all the necessary nuts/washers/bushes are present (at the top as well as the bottom). Depending on the car, the top mounts may be accessed from under the car or inside the boot or hatch. Once again, rubber bushes are used at each end of the shock absorber. When they wear excessively they become dangerous and are an MoT failure point.

Make sure that there are no signs of leakage from shock absorbers. With the amount of wet weather we get, it's often difficult to make out which is rain and which is leaking fluid. If you're unsure, wipe the shock absorber thoroughly and take the car for a short run. Even in wet weather, you should still be able to make out any fresh leakage on your return. The only an-

Bottom mounting of telescopic shock absorber.

swer if a leak is discovered is to replace the unit *AND* its opposite number on the other side of the axle. **Never** replace any 'paired' suspension components in 'ones.'

❏ COIL SPRINGS

It's important to check the road springs from the top to the bottom - it's easy to miss the top few coils because they're often awkward to see, especially at the front. The springs must be located correctly at top and bottom ends and be free from serious corrosion damage and evidence of attempted repair - it is not permissible or advisable to weld a broken spring. As part of the test, the car will be raised slightly on the ramp so as to decompress the springs: this will make any breaks more evident.

This spring is well and truly broken and would make the handling of the car 'interesting' to the point of being lethal!

❏ WHEEL BEARINGS

The wheel bearings are checked (front and rear) by 'rocking' the wheel by hand, first in one position

It's important to check the road springs from top to bottom ...

... as can be demonstrated by this picture.

and then using the same technique having spun the wheel through 180 degrees. When the wheel is turning, listen carefully for sounds of 'graunching', which indicates a bearing on the way out and in need of replacement. It is important to differentiate between play in the suspension components (kingpins, etc) and wheel bearing play. There should only be a very small, barely perceptible, amount of play in the wheel bearings. Warning! Don't put your hand under the wheel unless the vehicle is on axle stands.

Some wheel bearings are adjustable, others not: your workshop manual or handbook will advise

Checking wheel bearings.

about your own car.

Nowadays, front wheel drive cars are prevalent and the tester will make several checks. With the front wheels jacked up and the gearbox in neutral, he will rotate the wheels checking that the drive shafts are straight and damage-free and that the couplings at each

Check driveshaft gaiters carefully.

end of each shaft are in good condition and secure, with all mounting fasteners present and correct. With the steering on full lock he will rotate the wheels to ensure that the rubber gaiters are fully serviceable with no splits or damage: such failure is common. These gaiters protect finely machined bearings and joints which need to be immersed in grease in order to function correctly. If the gaiter is split and the grease escapes, the driveshaft will seize solid with disastrous consequences.

BRAKES

❏ SAFETY

When replacing brake shoes or pads it's advisable to use items which have no asbestos content. Asbestos dust is extremely harmful if inhaled and so care needs to be taken when you're working on your car's braking system. Unless you know for certain that the pads/shoes are asbestos-free, wear a mask and work carefully so as not to get too much dust into the air.

IMPORTANT NOTE: The braking system of any car is a vital safety feature. Do **NOT** work on any part of it unless you are justifiably confident in your abilities and have access to the right replacement parts and/or specialist tools where required. If you are unsure, take your car to a professional or, at the very least, get professional advice.

❏ CORROSION

Corrosion within 30cm (approx 12 inches) of any brake related item (for example, the parking brake lever and its mountings or the footbrake brake pedal itself) will attract the tester's attention - and a failure certificate to go with it. Don't forget that the 30cm rule applies in *all* directions.

❏ PARKING BRAKE (HANDBRAKE)

The object of the parking brake is that it should prevent at least two of the wheels from turning when it is applied (on a three-wheeled

Testing the parking brake.

vehicle, it must prevent at least one of the wheels from turning).

On most cars, the basic braking system is hydraulic in operation with the parking brake being mechanical, the lever usually pulling on two cables which manually operate the rear brakes. (On some rare models, the parking brake operates on the front wheels).

On cars with rear hydraulic disc brakes, there is often a separate set of brake shoes operated by the parking brake lever. It is important to consult your workshop manual before attempting any remedial work on your car's braking system.

Apply the parking brake in the car. If the lever can be pulled right to the top of its travel, then it is a failure point - the tester will always look for 'something in reserve.' Once the parking brake is in the 'on' position, the ratchet mechanism should work correctly - it should secure the lever in that position until the button on the end is used to release it. If it is possible to knock it to the 'off' position, it's a fail. Also check to make sure that there is no excessive lateral movement of the lever itself - the point here being, if the movement is enough, the cables could slip off, thus negating the braking effect. Some cars have

Typical handbrake adjusters.

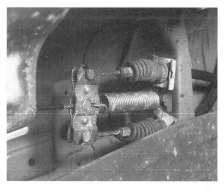

Check handbrake cables and linkages beneath car.

a 'fly-off' handbrake, which is on or off and nothing in between. In this case, its effectiveness will be checked in the same way and the

mechanism must work as originally intended.

If there is no reserve travel, it generally means that the hand-brake cables need adjusting. This is usually quite a simple task, with the adjusters of most cars being at either side of the handbrake lever inside the car - you may need to remove a cover. It is important to adjust them so that the brakes operate equally on each wheel. This will show up on the rolling road test at the MoT station. Check whether or not your handbrake is up to scratch by raising the wheels (don't forget the safety precautions) upon which the brake operates with the handbrake applied. It should not be possible to turn the wheels by hand.

If you can move a wheel a little, some adjustment is required. If there is no braking effect and the handbrake seems to be working correctly, there is a more serious problem. Depending on your car's braking system, it could be a seized calliper or handbrake cable, or totally worn shoes or a failed bearing spraying grease into the brake drum - the only way to find out, is to check further.

It's always advisable to have a look at the condition of the handbrake cables under the car. They take an awful lot of punishment from the elements, and it's very common to find that they have seized. The same principle applies if your car has a mechanical rod linkage. It is important to ensure that no parts of the handbrake linkages have rusted solid or become stiff. Sometimes, it is possible to free-off jammed components

Brake drum cable lever.

Check soundness of foot pedal rubber.

by using a releasing agent. In many cases, though, replacement is the only answer. While you're actually under the car looking at the cable/linkage, it's a good idea to take the grease tin and/or WD40 with you and make sure that all the moving/exposed parts get some lubrication. You can't be too careful!

The other common problem is that the cable lever inside the brake drum has rusted or seized solid. Again, this is a feature of its physical position in life, the effect of the elements and the fact that the parking brake is not used that often. It is quite possible for the parking brake to be working on one rear wheel only, and for the driver not to notice.

❏ SERVICE BRAKE (FOOTBRAKE)

Check your brake pedal rubber (and those of the accelerator and clutch, where appropriate). If your foot slips off any of the pedals, particularly the braked pedal, the results could be disastrous. Make sure that there are no obvious problems in the driver's side footwell, such as brake fluid leakages or faulty brake pedal/servo linkages.

THE SERVO

A car with a non-functioning servo fails the MoT test. In general, you'll know when your servo stops functioning, because suddenly your right leg muscles will need to work twice as hard in order to stop the car! This is because the servo uses vacuum from the intake manifold to halve (or more) the amount of foot pressure required for a given rate of retard.

TESTING THE SERVO

You can test your servo in the same way the tester will; with the ignition off, press and release the brake pedal a dozen times in rapid succession. Then hold the pedal down and start the engine - you should feel the pedal go down appreciably as the engine adds its weight

41

to your efforts. If there is no noticeable difference, then it points to servo trouble; it could be leaking vacuum lines or it could be that the servo has an internal fault and needs replacing.

Note that you should keep the pedal pressed down for around 15 seconds. If it goes down correctly but then continues its downward travel, it points to the possibility of an internal leak, for example, faulty hydraulic seals.

Under the bonnet, check that the servo itself is mounted securely and that all the various associated pipes and unions are secure. Look for splits and cracks in the pipes - bending a plastic or rubber pipe slightly will often reveal a split not immediately visible.

The tester will check all the braking components he can for general condition, including callipers. He will try to check on the condition of the brake pads (and shoes, if applicable). Ridiculous as it sounds, he is not even allowed to remove a wheel trim (as here) to ensure that the disc pads have plenty of 'meat' left on them. This does not apply to you, though, and you should be rigourous in

your visual examination.

The condition of the discs is vital when considering your car's braking system. A disc that is warped or scored (possibly through using worn pads) will not provide the stopping power you require. The front brakes always take more of the braking strain than the rear and if you have a 4-disc system, it's even possible that the rear callipers can seize-up without you noticing ...

Make regular checks on your brake pads. Pads which are worn right down make your car extremely dangerous, not to mention the fact that they will start to damage the brake disc itself. Shown at the left is a part worn pad - compare it to the new version alongside. Many pads have a groove down the centre (as here) which acts as a replacement guide - when the groove disappears, fit new pads.

Brake squeal isn't an MoT failure point in itself, but it's very annoying! Applying a copper-based grease to the *back* of the pads usually stops this problem. It's a good idea to apply a little to the threads of nuts and bolts as you replace them, in order to make them easier to remove next time. Take care, of course, not to get any oil or grease onto the pads, shoes, discs or drums.

Many cars have front disc brakes and drums at the rear. With the latter, it's usually the case that the shoes are replaced when necessary, but the ancillaries (slave cylinder, springs, washers etc) are ignored - but they don't have an infinite life, so if your car is any age, it's a good idea to be safe not sorry and replace the whole lot. The Bendix Kit-Plus package includes everything required to replace all the rear drum brake components and it comes with a comprehensive warranty.

Check that the brake fluid level is correct according to the marker on the side of the - usually transparent - reservoir. Some cars have a dipstick attached to the cap; whatever, there MUST be sufficient fluid

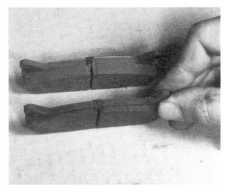

Brake pad wear.

in the system, otherwise, it's a fail. If it is a little below the mark, add some more fluid; it is normal for the level to go down *slightly* over a period of time because of brake pad wear, but a prodigious need for topping-up points to something seriously amiss in the hydraulic system. Take care not to get brake fluid on your hands or the car's paintwork; the fluid is harmful to paint unless it is of the silicone type, which also has the benefit of being non-hygroscopic - it doesn't attract the rust-forming moisture. To

Checking brake fluid level.

change, all the old fluid must be drained before replacing with silicone fluid and, of course, the brakes must be bled.

BRAKE PIPES

The condition of the brake pipes is vital. Check them underneath the car and in the engine bay, looking for any signs of corrosion, leakage or damage. Where a brake pipe should be clipped to the bodywork, then the clip must be in place - otherwise, it's a fail.

Checking the unions where metal/flexible pipes are interconnected is particularly important, as these are areas where leaks often occur. Unions around the steering area (pictured) are particularly prone to damage.

The best way to check a flexible brake pipe for leakage or damage is to bend it gently back like this. Cracks not otherwise obvious will often show themselves. If such a pipe is found to be

Check rigid brake pipes thoroughly.

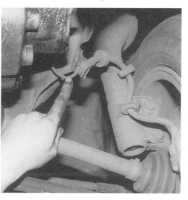

Check all unions.

Checking a flexible brake pipe for leakage.

cracked, replacement is required - quickly! As flexible pipes age, they tend to 'balloon' under pressure. Check this (very carefully!) by having an assistant operate the brake pedal while you watch the flexible pipe. Any evidence that the pipe is deforming as the brakes are applied means that a new pipe is required.

❏ THE BRAKE TEST

Testing stations are equipped with rolling brake machines, or decelerometers, which are able to measure braking efficiency. The percentage efficiency required will depend on whether your car has a dual or single braking system (see table on page 46).

The front brakes will usually be tested first. The wheels are placed in the rollers and, if a servo is fitted, the engine is started and left to idle. The service (foot) brake is applied until maximum efficiency is reached or until the tyre starts to slip. The right and left brakes are checked individually and the readings noted. Then, both rollers are started together. The tester will check that no braking effort is present whilst the brake pedal is not being applied (indicating that there is some constant drag, probably a sticking calliper) and then he will press the pedal as before, making sure that the braking effort from both wheels is reasonably even.

This procedure is then carried out on the rear wheels, for the service brake and the parking brake.

Where the efficiency is enough for a pass, but only just, the tester will inform the owner of that fact - clearly, in cases like this, it means that some work is due.

One of the most common faults revealed during the roller brake test is braking imbalance. Callipers are notorious for sticking on disc brakes and on the parking brake, the cables and levers are equally problematical. Other common problems are leaking slave cylinders on drum brakes (where the fluid is dripping onto the shoes and reducing the braking effect) and wheel bearing trouble, where the grease from the bearing gets onto the brake shoes.

* It's an important point to note that a roller brake test cannot be carried out on a vehicle with damaged, under-inflated or studded tyres.

* Whilst most cars can be tested on a standard roller brake tester, some cannot, notably those vehicles with:

        a) more than one driving axle permanently engaged
        b) a limited slip differential
        c) belt driven transmission
        d) brakes for which the servo oper

ates only when the vehicle is moving.

If your car falls in the categories, it will have to be tested on a decelerometer or plate brake tester.

Roller brakes, such as this one at Halfords, give the percentage braking efficiency figure directly on the dial.

Some brake testing machines record the readings in a format which then has to be cross-referenced on a scale to provide the efficiency readings required.

45

❏ BRAKE EFFICIENCY TABLE

The MoT requirements for braking efficiency are as follows (the most common type of vehicle being those in class 1);

CLASS OF VEHICLE	SERVICE BRAKE	PARKING BRAKE SINGLE BRAKING SYSTEM	SPLIT BRAKING SYSTEM
1. Vehicles with 4 or more wheels having a service brake (foot brake) operating on at least 4 wheels and a parking brake (handbrake) operating on at least 2 wheels.	50%	25%	16%
2. Vehicles with 3 wheels with a service brake operating on all wheels and a parking brake operating on at least one wheel which were first used:			
a) before 1st January 1968	40%	25%	16%
b) on or after 1st January 1968	50%	25%	16%
3. Vehicles first used before 1st January 1968 which do NOT have one means of control operating on at least 4 wheels (or 3 for 3-wheeled vehicles) and which have one brake system with 2 means of control or 2 brake systems with separate means of control.	30% from 1st means of control	25% from second means of control	
4. Vehicles first used before 1st January 1915	One efficient braking system required		

Note: 16% BRAKING EFFICIENCY EQUATES TO A VEHICLE HOLDING ON A GRADIENT OF 1 IN 6.25.

❏ ABS

ABS is the commonly accepted abbreviation for any form of anti-lock braking system. It should be noted that such systems are incredibly complex in their operation and service and/or repair should be left to the experts. Where an ABS system is fitted, a warning light (to show that it is not operative) will be fitted. Checking this is part of the MoT test and the device must be shown to be working correctly. Apart from the checking of the warning light, the brake tests carried out are the same as those for a standard hydraulic system.

ROAD WHEELS AND TYRES

❏ ROAD WHEELS

The road wheels will be tested along with the tyres. The tester is looking primarily to ensure that the wheels are secure and are not likely to fall. This means that there should be the prerequisite number of wheel bolts/studs and that they should be tight.

He will also check for potentially dangerous damage or distortion, e.g. heavy 'kerbing' or cracks caused by accident damage. Superficial damage will not be a cause for concern.

It is always advisable to use a torque wrench on road wheels bolts to avoid over tightening, especially when dealing with alloy wheels. Check your workshop manual or handbook for the torque figure required.

❏ TYRES

The examination of the tyres will take place of the road wheels only (i.e. not the spare). The tester will

Road wheels must be secure.

check each tyre in turn and will need to look at all of the tyre tread area, plus its inside and outside walls. He will be looking for bulges, cuts, foreign objects and adequate tread depth.

For all cars first used after 2nd January 1933, there must be a minimum of 1.6mm of tread over the centre 3/4 of the tyre tread pattern around the entire outer circumference of the tyre. Note that the 'tread pattern' does not include items such as wear bars, found on some tyres as visible indicators to show when replacement is due.

Though 1.6mm is an increase over the previous minimum (which was just 1mm for many years) it still isn't much tread and the braking distances for such tyres, when compared with

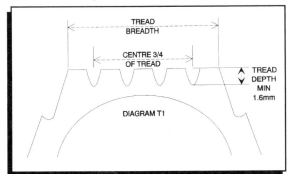

Tyre tread depth requirements.

tyres with 3mm or more, are considerably longer.

A 1.0mm minimum tread depth applies to passenger carrying vehicles with more than 8 passenger seats (excluding the driver's seat) or vehicles first used before 3rd January 1993.

The tester will check the details

Check that tyre types are compatible.

on the side of the tyre to ensure that the tyres are compatible. On a 3 or 4 wheeled vehicle, you *must not* mix:

1. Tyres of a different structure on the same axle.

Checking tread depth.

2. Cross ply or bias belted tyres on the front axle and radial ply on the rear.

3). Cross ply on the rear axle and bias belted on the front axle.

It is permissible to mix radial ply tyres of both fabric and steel construction at will.

Checking the depth of your tyre's tread is easy - use a depth tread gauge. This almost new tyre shows around 8mm of tread and is well inside the MoT test minimum of 1.6mm.

If you find your car's tyre wear is uneven, it could be caused by any one (or combination of) factors; incorrect inflation, worn suspension components or badly adjusted tracking. If it's the latter, Gunson's produce a device called the Trakrite which gives a good guide as to whether your wheels are pointing where they should be. Check your workshop manual for tracking adjustment procedures and settings.

The tyre pressures are not part of the test, unless they are so obviously low that to drive the car would make it a danger on the road. Tyre wear problems (uneven wear, etc) can be a cause of failure and incorrect inflation rates are often the cause. You're well advised to invest in a quality tester like the one illustrated from the author's tool box. It's over 20 years old and has more than paid back its small initial cost. Gauges at many garages are inaccurate, largely because of the unsympathetic treatment they get from some members of

Trakrite device.

the public.

The condition of the spare tyre is not part of the test, but if a defect is found (as here - there's hardly any tread on this tyre!) the tester will report the tyre to the car's owner with the obvious advice that it should be rectified. Naturally, in the event of a puncture, fitting a bald or badly damaged tyre will result in the car becoming instantly illegal - the maximum penalties at the time of writing were 3 penalty points and a £2,500 fine!

Checking tyre pressure.

SEAT BELTS

The test applies only to vehicles first used on or after 1st January 1965 and only to *mandatory* belts - those required to be fitted in the car by law. Any belts fitted as 'optional extras' may be checked, but any faults discovered will not be the cause of a failure certificate, though the owner will be informed and should seek to effect rectification of the faults.

❏ ALL PRESENT & CORRECT
The tester's first task is to make sure that the correct number and type of seat belts are present for the age and type of car. The tables and diagrams included in this chapter show what he is looking for and what you should have.

❏ SEAT BELT REQUIREMENTS FOR VEHICLES FIRST USED ON OR AFTER 1ST JANUARY 1965 AND BEFORE 1ST APRIL 1987

VEHICLE DESCRIPTION
1. Passenger vehicles
- with 4 or more wheels
- with up to 12 passenger seats
- first used on or after 1st January 1965

2. 3-Wheeled vehicles
- with an unladen weight over 410kgs first used on or after 1st January 1965 or
- with an unladen weight over 225 kgs if first used on or after

1st September 1970
Except vehicles:

- *less than 410kgs unladen, equipped with a driving seat of a type requiring the driver to sit astride it and*
- *constructed or assembled by a person not ordinarily engaged in the trade or business of manufacturing vehicles of this type.*

3. Goods vehicles, motor caravans and ambulances
- with an unladen weight not exceeding 1525kgs
- first used on or after 1st April 1967

4. Goods vehicles, motor caravans and ambulances
- with a design gross weight not exceeding 3500kgs
- first used on or after 1st April 1980

except those first used before 1st April 1982, if they are of a model manufactured before 1st October 1979 with an unladen weight exceeding 1525kgs.

DRIVER'S & SPECIFIED FRONT PASSENGER'S SEAT
Vehicles first used before 1st April 1981:
- A belt which restrains the upper part of the body (but need not include a lap belt) for each seat.

Vehicles first used after 31st March 1981:

- A 3-point (lap/diagonal) belt **

NOTE 1

THE 'SPECIFIED FRONT PASSENGER'S SEAT' REQUIRING A SEAT BELT IS THE SEAT WHICH IS; FOREMOST IN THE VEHICLE AND FURTHEST FROM THE DRIVER'S SEAT UNLESS THERE IS A FIXED PARTITION SEPARATING THE PASSENGER SEAT FROM A SPACE IN FRONT OF IT WHICH IS ALONGSIDE THE DRIVER'S SEAT, EG. CERTAIN TYPES OF TAXIS, BUSES ETC.

**NOTE 2*

A 3-POINT BELT MEANS A SEAT BELT WHICH
- RESTRAINS THE UPPER AND LOWER PARTS OF THE TORSO
- INCLUDES A LAP BELT
- IS ANCHORED AT NOT LESS THAN THREE POINTS AND
- IS DESIGNED FOR USE BY AN ADULT.

CENTRE FRONT SEAT
- No requirement.

FORWARD FACING REAR SEATS
- No requirement.

❏ SEAT BELT REQUIREMENTS FOR VEHICLES FIRST USED AFTER 31ST MARCH 1987

VEHICLE DESCRIPTION

1. Passenger vehicles and dual purpose vehicles with not more than 8 passenger seats.

DRIVER'S & SPECIFIED FRONT PASSENGER'S SEAT
- 3-point belts for each seat.**

CENTRE FRONT SEAT
- 3-point belt**, lap belt or disabled persons belt.

FORWARD FACING REAR SEATS
- See accompanying dia-

gram (page 52).

2. Goods Vehicles

DRIVER'S & SPECIFIED FRONT PASSENGER'S SEAT
- As above

CENTRE FRONT SEAT
- As above

FORWARD FACING REAR SEATS
- No requirement

3. Vehicles first used before 1st October 1988 which are:
- Minibuses with up to 12 passenger seats
- Motor caravans and ambulances with a design gross weight not exceeding 3500kgs

DRIVER'S & SPECIFIED FRONT PASSENGER'S SEAT
- As above

CENTRE FRONT SEAT
- No requirement

FORWARD FACING REAR SEATS
- No requirement

4. Minibuses, motor caravans and ambulances:
- With a design gross weight not exceeding 3500kgs
- First used after 31st September 1988

DRIVER'S & SPECIFIED FRONT PASSENGER'S SEAT
- As above

CENTRE FRONT SEAT
- 3-point belt or a lap belt

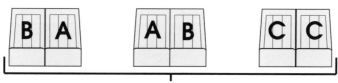

Two forward facing rear seats. Seatbelts can be in any of the above combinations.

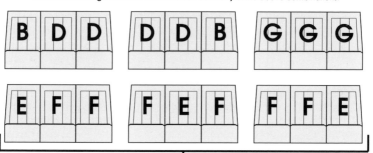

Three forward facing rear seats. Seatbelts can be in any of the above combinations.

Note:
- Rear or side facing seats are not required to be fitted with seatbelts.
- Rear seat seatbelts are not required in any vehicle with more than eight seats (excluding the driver's seat).

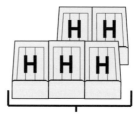

More than three forward facing rear seats.

A: No belts required.
B: 3 point inertia reel.
C: Each of these seats with either a lap belt, child restraint belt, disabled person's belt or 3 point static belt.
D: One of these adjacent seats with either a lap belt, child restraint belt, disabled person's belt or a 3 point belt (static or inertia reel).
E: 3 point static belt.
F: One of the two 'F' seats with either a child restraint belt or a disabled persons belt.
G: Each of the three 'G' seats with (in any combination) either a lap belt, child restraint belt, disabled person's belt or 3 point belt (inertia or static).
H: Acceptable belts are lap belts, disabled person's belts, child restraint belts or 3 point belts (inertia reel or static). There are three seatbelt options -
• Option one: if one outboard (seats closest to the vehicle sides) has a 3 point inertia reel type belt, then at least one other seat must have an acceptable belt.
• Option two: if any seat has a 3 point static belt, then at least one other seat must have either a child restraint belt or a disabled person's belt.
• Option three: if no seat has a 3 point (inertia reel or static) belt, then EACH seat must have an acceptable belt.

Seat belt requirements for rear seats of vehicles first used after 31st March 1987.

 • No requirement

❑ WEBBING CHECKS

Check the condition of the belts themselves; you're looking for worn webbing, cuts or frayed stitching, all of which could be dangerous. Make sure you pull all the belt out and look very carefully indeed for any signs of wear. Like all parts on any car, the seat belts

Check operation of seat belt clasps.

deteriorate with age and unfortunately, a destruction test is the only way to be absolutely sure that a belt is truly up to scratch. As such, *any* sign of wear or damage means that the belts must be replaced - certainly, they'll fail the test. The belts must be fully operative. An inertia reel belt must retract correctly, *i.e.* when extended and released it should return smoothly and easily into the mechanism..

It is permissible to give a little help, but if it does not retract completely, then it needs replacing.

In addition, the operation of the inertia ratchet mechanism should be checked by giving a sharp tug to the belt to ensure that (where applicable) it locks up. (Some seat belt systems are linked to sub-systems and pre-tensioning devices - check with the vehicle manufacturer if you are in any doubt as to the safety and/or checking methods).

Fasten the seat belt at the buckle and then release it. For obvious reasons, it is important that the buckle should release instantly and eagerly. Any hesitation could indi-

cate a possible fault - replace the belt if you are in any doubt, as it is not only an MoT failure point, but also it is potentially extremely dangerous.

The belts and anchorages must

Check seatbelt mountings for security.

53

be securely fastened to the car, but bear in mind some anchors are designed to swivel - all necessary bolts must be present and tightened as required and all spacers/washers etc. should be present and correct. As with most items on your car, there is a torque figure to adhere to - check your manual. It is possible for flexible buckle stalks to be damaged internally, a fault recognisable by listening for a clicking noise as the stalk is moved from side to side. The rule with regard to corrosion of load bearing parts of the car applies here. There should be no serious corrosion or fracture or other damage within 30 cm (approx 12 inches) of any seat belt anchorage - front or rear. This also applies to the actual seat mounting, where a belt anchorage forms part of the seat itself. In the latter case, the seat will be inspected even more thoroughly than usual and the actual framework of the seat will come in for some close scrutiny. It's not likely that you'll see much

Replacing a seat belt is not difficult, requiring only the tools to be found in the average workshop. Neither is it particularly expensive as companies like Securon can usually supply all kinds of belt and with the same quality as those supplied by the vehicle manufacturer.
Look long and hard at your belts once they are five years old (especially if they've led a hard life) and consider replacing ten year old belts as a matter of course - in the front at least. Don't stint here and don't count the cost - lives could depend on them.

corrosion inside the car, but you should look all the same - better safe than sorry. However, it is something which forms a major item in your under-vehicle checks.

GENERAL ITEMS

❏ THE DRIVER'S VIEW OF THE ROAD

This heading now covers the windscreen as well as the washers and wipers. First things first, you should make sure your windscreen is clean. If it's not, you might miss an important crack or chip.

The requirement is that drivers must be able to see the road ahead clearly. This means that the windscreen must be sufficiently free of obstructions, cracks and splits within designated areas and that there should be some method of cleaning it when dirty - windscreen wipers and washers, both operated from inside the vehicle. Indeed, it is an offence to have a dirty windscreen.

❏ WINDSCREEN CHECKS

The tester will look at that part of the windscreen swept by the wiper blades and divide his inspection into two parts; firstly, zone 'A' and then the rest of the swept area (see accompanying illustration.

Zone 'A' is 290mm wide, within the swept area of the screen and centred on the steering wheel. It should have no damaged area

larger than 10mm, no stickers or other obstructions infringing the area by more than 10mm NOR a number of smaller areas of damage which combine to impede the drivers' vision in a serious manner - for example, an old windscreen which has been 'peppered' over the years by flying stones etc. The test is more lenient with damage occurring within the swept area but outside zone 'A' - a chip or crack is only a failure point if it cannot be contained within a 40mm diameter circle.

The tester will have a plastic gauge with 10mm and 40mm diameter holes in it. This makes it a simple task to check the screen.

STICKERS

In general, no stickers should appear within the swept area. The

Windscreen areas swept by wipers and zone 'A'.

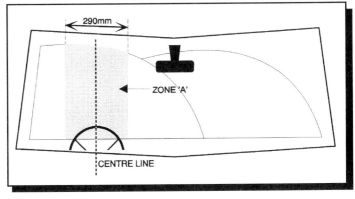

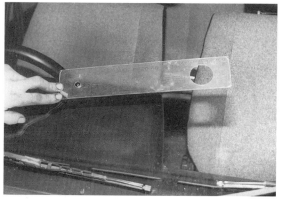

You can make your own windscreen legality gauge by using the diagram here as a template. Simply transfer it onto a piece of stiff card (or even clear plastic, if you have any) and keep it in your glovebox. If you're unsure as to whether your screen is legal or not, almost all windscreen replacement centres offer a free pre-MoT check.

exceptions are official stickers (such as a tax disc or parking permit) as long as they do not seriously impede the driver's view of the road.

EXCEPTION TO THE RULE

All vehicles are subject to the windscreen test except those with opening windscreens or those with another means of providing the driver with an adequate view of the road. Effectively, vehicles meeting these descriptions are likely to be particularly old or unusual.

WINDSCREEN REPAIRS

Many windscreen replacement companies (and some specialists) are now advertising repair services. It must be noted however, that any reputable repairer will work only to the British Standard, BS AU242. Part and parcel of this is that NO WINDSCREEN THAT WOULD FAIL THE MoT CAN BE REPAIRED.

Some windscreens can be repaired, but the repair will be effected to aprevent any damage from spreading and to improve the driver's view of the road.

In order to ensure some kind of safe uniformity, BS (British Stand-

PASS YOUR MoT
WINDSCREEN CHECKER

**10mm limit
zone 'A'**

**40mm limit
rest of
swept area**

Official stickers (tax discs etc) are permitted as long as they do not seriously obstruct the driver's vision.

ard) AU242 recommends that the following rules are followed:

* Repairs are never to be effected in zone 'A' (see diagram); because repairs can never be totally effective, there is the risk that, in certain circumstances, some loss of visibility could occur. As zone 'A' is directly in front of the driver, it is considered unsafe to take this risk.

* Repairs in the portion of the screen swept by the driver's wiper blade which does not come under zone 'A' can be carried out up to a maximum diameter of 15mm.

* Repairs in the area swept by passenger wiper blade can be repaired where the damage can be contained within a 25mm diameter circle.

* No damage on the rest of the screen can be repaired if it represents a circle with a diameter of more than 40mm.

The benefit in repair rather than replace is mainly a financial one; most comprehensive insurance policies carry a £40+ excess - that part of the total windscreen cost that the car owner has to pay. Moreover, if the driver has only third-party or third-party fire and theft cover (and has not taken any windscreen option) then the full cost of the windscreen falls to him. At present, the average windscreen cost is around £145! However, almost all insurance companies will pay the total cost of repairing a screen (currently running at an average of £35), without imposing an excess or affecting the no-claims discount; obviously, it's in their interest, as it could save them around £100 a claim.

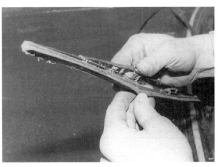

Check condition of wiper blades.

Check that there is fluid in the windscreen washer bottle.

❏ **WINDSCREEN WIPERS AND WASHERS**

The wipers should be in good condition and maintain contact with the screen throughout their arc. Having been switched on, they should continue to wipe - ie, they should not be intermittent in their operation unless, of course, intermittent mode is available and selected.

The washers must provide a water jet which, in conjunction with the wiper action, is sufficient to clear the screen.

It's important to ensure that the water bottle is topped up - even though the washers work, you'll still get a failure certificate if there's no water to feed them! It's always a good idea to add some windscreen cleaner, which also acts as a de-icing agent in bad weather as well.

If the jets don't spray correctly onto the screen or their operation is sporadic, check that the spray nozzles are clear and angled correctly - you gain no points for cleaning the screen of the car behind! Most spray nozzles can be cleaned and adjusted by using a household pin. Technically, it is only a requirement for the driver's side washer to be functional, BUT given the requirement for the driver to be able to see clearly through the whole screen, a faulty passenger-side washer would almost certainly result in a 'fail.'

In general, electric water pumps are very effective, but some vehicles rely on pneumatic pumps which are, on occasion, operated from the spare tyre. You should ensure that there is sufficient pressure available before the test. Those older washers which rely on a driver operated plunger or foot operated bellows can fail if the one-way valve in the washer bottle is faulty.

REARSCREEN WIPERS
Rear screen wipers do not form part of the test, unless they are poorly secured and could be regarded as dangerous bodywork.

❏ AUDIBLE WARNING
HORN
All vehicles must have a method of providing an audible warning to other road users and the control switch (usually a pad - or pads - on the steering wheel) must be easily accessible by the driver and be fully functional. The tester will expect the horn to sound a constant note and be loud enough to attract attention. The rules also state that a horn on a vehicle first used on or after 1st August 1973 must not make a harsh or grating sound. It's a subject of some debate as to exactly what that means and heads rapidly in the direction of 'grey areas.'

TWO TONE HORNS
Two-tone horns are permissible, BUT the tones must sound together; a horn which produces alternate tones at regular intervals will result in a failure, largely because they could be mistaken for the sirens used by the emergency services.

SIRENS
A siren can be fitted to any car, but must only be used as part of an anti-theft device, not as the means of providing audible warning whilst the car is on the move. (This rule also applies to bells and gongs!)

It is not unusual to find that the horn terminals have become a little corroded, meaning that the horn either doesn't work or is a little tardy in its operation. Removing the horn pad and applying a little emery paper to the terminals usually does the trick. If there is still no sound, check the horn itself, which is usually mounted behind the lower front valance of the car. It leads a hard life and it is possible that one of the terminals has come adrift or corrosion is causing a problem.

Clean the terminals with emery cloth - treating them with a copper-based grease is a good idea - and ensure that they are a tight fit on the horn. If there is still no sound and you have used your test light to check that the horn is receiving power and that the switch is operating correctly, it must be assumed that the horn is faulty and a new one is required.

EXCEPTION TO THE RULE

Vehicles designed before 1st January 1905 and constructed before 31st December 1905 are allowed to have a bell, gong or siren as its sole means of audible warning. Not a rule which will apply to many of us!

❏ EXHAUST
SAFETY

Never work on your exhaust system when it is hot - for obvious reasons! Exhaust gasses are always unpleasant and poisonous and can kill within minutes. Whenever you're working on your car and need to have the engine running, do so outside - even working with the garage door wide open may not be enough to be totally safe.

CATALYTIC CONVERTERS

Remember that catalytic converters work at much higher temperatures than 'normal' systems and should be treated with even more respect. In particular, you should always be careful not to park your car over flammable materials. Use some care when checking catalyst equipped exhaust systems, for they are easy to damage and, in some cases, this can lead to them producing more pollution than if a 'normal' exhaust were fitted!

VISUAL & AURAL CHECK

You can make a visual and aural check of your exhaust from the outside (prior to your check underneath). You can make sure that the rear mounting rubbers are present and in good condition.

These rubbers can deteriorate quite badly for after a while, the rubber stretches and becomes brittle, allowing the exhaust system to rattle against the underside of the vehicle or suspension components or, in extreme cases, scrape along the road surface.

Be assured, no tester will pass an exhaust system held on by bits of wire.

Most exhaust support rubbers cost very little from an exhaust/tyre specialist. Put on your thick gloves and grab hold of the end of the exhaust pipe (while it's cold, of course) giving it a good waggle. If all is well, you shouldn't hear much in the way of 'clunking'. Lots of clattering is a sign that all is not well - make a note for when you get under the car.

Start the engine (in the open air - NOT in your garage!) and walk around the car; you will be able to hear any major leaks as flat, 'woofling' sounds. It sometimes helps to briefly cover the end of the exhaust to highlight the sounds of leaking gasses elsewhere. (Not with your bare hand on a hot exhaust pipe, of course.)

trian. It is true to say that if there is serious damage at this point, the back section of the exhaust probably needs replacing anyway.

A DIY repair to part of an exhaust system will not necessarily mean a failure, though it must be very secure. Minor leaks will also not be cause for failure, given that there is not excessive noise, though the tester will take into account the condition of the system as a whole; if it is clearly on its last legs, any leaks and noise can only get worse, and he would probably fail it. Conversely, any minor leaks on a virtually new system will, before long, probably seal themselves with the soot from the exhaust gasses.

Holes in the exhaust pipe after the last silencer box would not normally result in a fail. However, if the hole and/or corrosion is bad enough, it might come under the heading of unsafe bodywork, in that it might endanger other road users if it were to fall off or injure a pedes-

There are many and various designs of rubber exhaust mountings but the rubber 'O' ring version is the most common. All types of rubber mountings will deteriorate slowly, allowing the exhaust system to wallow around, knocking against the underside of the car. The sign of a rubber that is on its way out is that it shows cracks when it is stretched or folded. Replacement is the only answer.

❏ EXHAUST EMISSIONS (PETROL ENGINES)

The amount of CO (carbon monoxide) your car emits through its

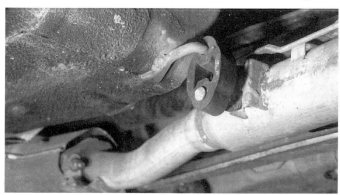

Typical rubber O-ring exhaust mounting.

exhaust is a subject of the MoT test. Though the testing station checks this to the prescribed limits using very expensive equipment, there are some very accurate DIY products available enabling you to check your own car exhaust emissions.

An engine in good condition and in the right state of tune will waltz through the exhaust emission tests. You can take some obvious pointers without opening the bonnet.

If your car's fuel consumption has been getting heavier lately, and/or you've found the car's performance to be noticeably worse in terms of acceleration and top speed, the odds are your engine is going 'off tune'. Equally, take a look at the end of your exhaust pipe immediately after a run of a few miles. If it is black and sooty, the engine is running too rich and emitting far too much CO.

Two typical engine analysers used to tune engines correctly.

With your engine tuned correctly, you will not only stand a good chance of getting through emissions test, but also, you'll be saving money (in terms of less fuel used) and enjoying your motoring more with a lively and better performing engine.

Modern motorists can tune their cars very accurately by using one of the latest engine analysers - hand-held devices which offer almost as much information about the state of the engine's tune as many machines costing thousands of pounds.

The tester will want to see that the vehicle does not emit dense blue, or clearly visible black, smoke for a continuous period of 5 seconds whilst the engine is at idling speed. Where an engine will not idle at a reasonable speed, it is possible for it to be a failure point - there are cases of owners raising the speed in order to artificially prevent excess smoke. If the car was first used prior to 1st August 1975, this visual check is the ONLY one made.

In the case of cars first used after the 1st August 1975, the CO (carbon monoxide) output and hydrocarbon content of the car's exhaust emissions will be measured. Hydrocarbons are measured in parts per million (ppm) and CO is referred to as a percentage (%) figure.

In order to allow for the fact that cars have become ever 'cleaner' over recent years (thanks in no small part to the advances in vehicle electronics and engine management systems) younger cars have a stricter criteria to adhere to as the accompanying table shows.

MODIFIED VEHICLES

In addition, if your car's engine has been seriously modified (for exam- sive testing equipment, it is possible for the DIY motorist to check his car's exhaust emissions. Gunson's

Vehicle age	Hydrocarbons PPM	Carbon Monoxide (CO)
Vehicles first used before 1st August 1975	Visual excessive smoke check only	
Vehicles first used on or after 1st August 1975	1200	6%
Vehicles first used on or after 1st August 1983	1200	4.5%

NOTE: Kit cars, vehicles constructed by amateurs and vehicles powered by Wankel rotary engines (first used before 1st August 1987) are all considered to be vehicles first used before 1st August 1975 for the purpose of the exhaust emissions test.

ple, if it has been rebored to a higher capacity and fitted with an uprated camshaft), then it may well be exempt from the above regulations. If you feel that your car comes under this heading, you should contact your local MoT garage and seek their opinion. Take with you any proof you have of the extent of the modifications. Whatever you do, don't wait until the car is on the ramps with the exhaust analyser at the ready before you mention it.

It should be noted that exhaust gas measurements are taken with an engine that has been fully warmed up. The engine will then be revved to 2,500rpm (or half the engine's maximum speed if it is lower) and held there for around 20 seconds in order to 'purge' the inlet and exhaust systems and reduce the chance of a false reading. The reading will then be taken over a 5 second period.

Despite the fact that MoT testing stations use complex and expen-

produce a pair of DIY gastesters which, in our experience, produce impressively accurate results. Their cost is reasonable (and certainly nowhere near the thousands of

Exhaust gas analysis during an MoT test.

Gunson's DIY gastesters are, in our experience, impressively accurate. The model shown here is the top-of-the-range Professional, which features a digital display readout and can also be used to measure ohms, dwell angle and rpm in order to assist with the perfect tuning of your engine.

pounds required for the equipment found in most garages), particularly if a failure and retest is avoided. It becomes even cheaper if the machine is bought as a 'cooperative' venture say as part of a club or with a friend or neighbour (or two!).

❏ EXHAUST EMISSIONS
(DIESEL ENGINES)

Regulations to test emissions from diesel-engined cars were first introduced in 1993, but swiftly dropped when it became apparent that they were going to be troublesome - several engines were blown up during the test! After a year's absence, they reappeared in 1994 and apply to all diesel powered cars manufactured on or after 1st August 1979.

The test is not to check the emissions as on a petrol-engined car (they are too low) but rather to measure the levels of smoke from the exhaust using specially designed electronic equipment. (To date, there are no DIY versions of this machinery). In essence, the 'thickness' of smoke is measured

over a number of runs at the maximum governed engine speed (the main changes to the testing procedure involved reducing the amount of time the engine spends at maximum speed and the number of test cycles). It is important to note that the DoT take no responsibility for engines damaged during the procedure. Their view is that "...the test procedure will present no threat to a properly maintained engine. If the motorist is in any doubt about the general condition of their diesel vehicle they should have it serviced before the MoT test, rather than run the slight risk of damage occurring during the test." You have been warned! As well as making sure that your engine is in a good state of tune, it's a good idea to perform an oil change before the test. If you can, ask to watch the test being carried out (most Halfords centres, for example, have specially designed viewing areas) which means you can make sure that the smoke test is not carried out with a cold engine. The standard to be met is the same as that for heavy goods vehicles and buses, *i.e:*

Non-turbocharged engines	3.2m
Turbocharged engines	3.7m

❏ STRUCTURAL INTEGRITY & CORROSION

SAFETY FIRST & INTRODUCTION

In order to check most of the areas mentioned here, you'll need to be under the car. Naturally, this means raising it in some way and so you must take extreme care. Refer to the safety comments at the front of the book before undertaking the work described here.

In addition, don't forget that any car's undersides will be covered with dirt and (possibly) flaking rust. Protect your eyes with goggles as a matter of course and use strong gloves to prevent cuts and grazes.

In order to assess the affect of any corrosion on the underside of your vehicle, refer to the three accompanying diagrams. These show (by means of shaded sections) the officially prescribed areas which give a vehicle most of its strength. Whichever type of structure your vehicle has, ALL parts of the structure denoted by the shaded areas must be structurally sound. In addition, those parts of the structure to which testable items are mounted (*e.g.* steering rack mounting area) and areas within 30cm (approx 12 inches) of these points must be structurally sound.

When checking, you need to look at any area supporting (in any way) components relating to the braking, steering, suspension, seats and seat belt mountings of the car.

Typical one-piece chassis or integral subframe structure showing 'prescribed areas' in grey.

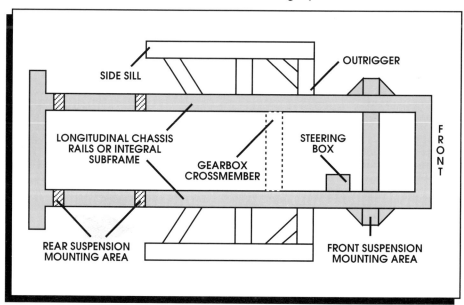

SIDE SILL

OUTRIGGER

LONGITUDINAL CHASSIS RAILS OR INTEGRAL SUBFRAME

GEARBOX CROSSMEMBER

STEERING BOX

FRONT

REAR SUSPENSION MOUNTING AREA

FRONT SUSPENSION MOUNTING AREA

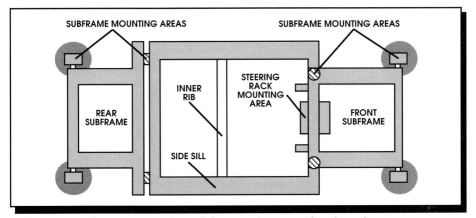

Some cars have separate subframes to carry front and rear suspension. 'Prescribed areas' are shown in grey.

REPAIRS

It is not satisfactory for corroded or weak metal to be repaired by using filler and/or fibreglass(*i.e.* GRP - glass reinforced plastic). Neither is brazing and/or soldering suitable; repairs to metal in prescribed areas *must* be carried out by welding.

Where corrosion has weakened a metal structure, though not enough to warrant a failure certifi-

Typical modern monocoque construction. Prescribed areas' are shown in grey.

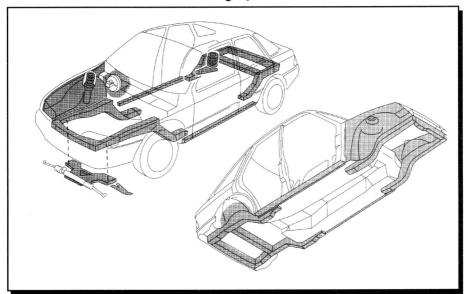

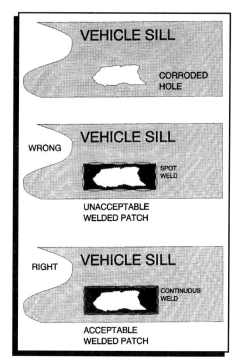

Figure shows three panels labeled VEHICLE SILL:
- Top: CORRODED HOLE
- Middle: WRONG — SPOT WELD — UNACCEPTABLE WELDED PATCH
- Bottom: RIGHT — CONTINUOUS WELD — ACCEPTABLE WELDED PATCH

MoT welded repair requirements.

part of the original design.

NON-METALLIC LOAD BEARING STRUCTURES

On occasion, it might be found that a testable item (such as a seat belt mounting or steering rack) is affixed to a plastic structure. If the manufacturer* built it that way, then it must be have been deemed to be strong enough when new. The tester will be looking to make sure that it has not deteriorated in any way, by cracking etc. Repairs to such parts in a prescribed area and/or which affect a load-bearing structure must be as strong as the original. Kit cars built by an amateur may not come under this ruling. The tester will use his judgment as to the safety and advisability of plastic structures.

The rules as to what a tester can and cannot do when checking for excessive corrosion are very strict. He cannot, as many think, go around the car with a 7lb lump hammer, thumping away until a panel gives way! In fact, the only

The officially approved 'Toffee Hammer'.

cate, the tester will point it out to the vehicle owner.

WELDING

Welding is an art form and nowhere near as simple as a professional makes it look. In general, DIY electric arc welding will be difficult to effect to a suitably high standard, not least because it tends to be a little fierce for the relatively thin metal of most car bodywork. Certainly, where safety related items are concerned, it is advisable to approach a professional. Any welded repairs must use replacement metal (or metal parts) of a suitable gauge (thickness) - the object is, of course, to make the repair as strong as the original structure. Welded seams must be continuous unless 'spot' welds were

Using 'Toffee Hammer' to test underside of a Volvo.

tool the tester is allowed to use is a small officially-approved combined hammer/scraper, known within the trade as the 'toffee hammer' - for obvious reasons. Its official title is 'The Corrosion Assessment Tool'

The hammer comprises a durable engineering plastic head for

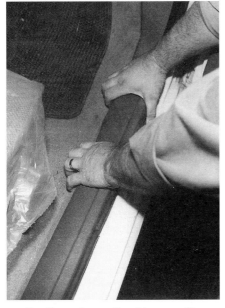

Testing strength of inner sills.

light tapping and an aluminium alloy shaft with a curved 'spade end' for light scraping. The alloy shaft can also be used as a lever. When seeking out corrosion under the car, the tester is allowed only to tap with the hammer end. In general, it is not necessary for him to find a hole - good metal resonates, whereas rust just creates a dull thud

when struck. Equally, a fibreglassed area sounds different to metal, and there are many areas under the car which must be metal for safety's sake. As such, they have to be repaired by welding and in NO other way.

(The only exception with the use of the 'toffee hammer' is in areas

It's an interesting point that where the sill is covered by some form of body addenda, whether a single piece trim like this, or as part of a complete body kit, the outer sill cannot be inspected - the tester is not allowed to remove anything to check what's underneath.

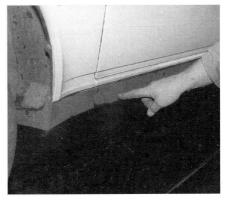

inaccessible to it, whereupon a small screwdriver may be used.)

The sills, inner and outer, are vital to the structural integrity of the car. Checking the sills inside the car, the tester will squeeze to see if the sill gives way under the pressure of his grip. He is not allowed to lift any carpets to see what is underneath. The sills are typical of many steel

The front suspension turret of cars with strut-type suspension is prone to corrosion which can often be seen from under the bonnet. Remove the rubber/plastic cap (where fitted) and have a good look around. Signs of surface rust (as here), do not necessarily mean that there will be serious corrosion. However, rust should be treated as soon as possible with an anti-rust agent to prevent future problems. Where the corrosion is more serious, it could result in a fail.

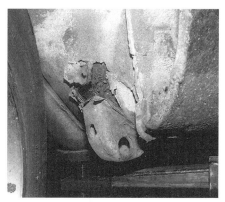

A typical but serious problem. On this Cortina water has become trapped under aging layers of underseal and has gradually eaten away metal This amount of corrosion is a definite fail and would have to be repaired by welding. This particular area is one to check on all cars as stones thrown up from the front wheels tend to damage the paint and/or underseal, thus exposing the bare metal to the elements. Some cars have plastic undershields fitted by the manufacturers to prevent this kind of damage. The tester is not allowed to remove this to check for corrosion underneath, but you'd be wise to do this yourself in your pre-MoT checks just to make sure - you can't be too careful ...

pressings in that they are hollow. This means that moisture gets trapped inside and eats away the metal from the inside out. It's a good idea to drill a hole in the top of the sill (under the carpet inside the vehicle) and inject Waxoyl or similar directly in order to slow down the onslaught of rust. A rubber bung (of the sort used for filling unwanted radio aerial holes in a wing) should be used to plug the hole. In addition, some hollow sections have drain holes in order to prevent rust forming. However,

Similarly, the rear suspension spring/shock absorber turrets suffer much the same fate as front turrets and can usually be viewed from inside the hatch or boot.

these can get blocked with road dirt etc., and it's advisable to check and clean them out with wire on a regular basis.

❑ BODYWORK CONDITION

The area of bodywork condition is one strewn with 'grey areas' and is one where the skill and experience of the tester comes into play. In essence, he is looking to ensure that there are no areas of excessive corrosion or damage resulting is dangerous and what isn't. So, if you're in any doubt, call in at your MoT garage before the test and ask.

❑ DOOR LOCKS

One of the later additions to the MoT test is the condition

No need to go underneath the car to see that the rot has well and truly set in on this Escort floor, running in a line from the hatch to beyond the rear seats. Its close proximity to the suspension components would make this a failure point.

in exposed sharp edges likely to cause injury to pedestrians. As you will see from the photos, it's not always immediately obvious what

Corrosion here, at the rear of this spare wheel well, has holed the metal. However, as it is not an area with safety considerations and is unlikely to cause major problems, it does not constitute a failure point.

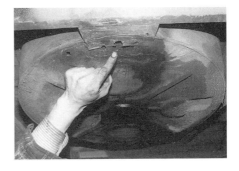

This is a fail - no question. The plastic bumper corner is missing, leaving those sharp brackets and screws exposed and ready to cause injury.

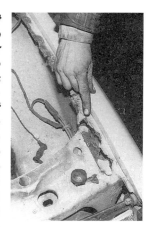

A little rust along the top of the inner wing inside the bonnet is not uncommon. It's not a problem unless the corrosion is so bad as to bring the security of the wing into question.

and effective operation of door latches.

EXCEPTION TO THE RULE

Exceptions to latching requirements are made where a vehicle does not have door handles as part of its original design characteristics or where it has been heavily customised. For example, it is very common for customisers to remove outer door handles/locks altogether in order to present a totally 'clean' face to the world. (In cases like this, the owners tend to rely on electronic remotely-operated central locking to gain access to the vehicle.) The key point is that the doors must be capable of being

Now here's a borderline case. This wing has a hole corroded in its top edge. If it were actually on the side of the wing, it could instantly be regarded as a fail because it could endanger other road users even when the car was parked - the sharp, corroded edges could injure a pedestrian. However, when the rusted area is as shown here, it is more open to interpretation. It's a case for the judgement of the tester who will doubtless relate this problem to the condition of the rest of the car. It should be noted that the owner of this car could remove any doubt about this particular point by filling the hole with fibreglass/filler etc. Because it is not a load-bearing item, this would be acceptable and as long as the repair was carried out efficiently, the tester would have no hesitation in passing it.

Another tricky one for the tester. The lower part of this Escort door has corroded to the extent that it can actually be pulled away almost half an inch. Clearly, there's plenty of corrosion, but should it be failed? How would it harm a member of the public? At first glance, it would appear that the person most at risk would be an unsuspecting passenger getting in or out of the car, however, further investigation showed that the lower door was also adrift at the front of the car and, moreover, when the car was moving, the effect of the moving air beneath it was to raise the section outwards like a wing. Now this would be a serious danger to a pedestrian for, it could act as a sythe. Verdict? Fail!

The tester will ensure that all doors on the car can be latched securely, ie. they are not liable to fly open without warning whilst the car is moving. He will also check that the FRONT doors can be opened from the outside and the inside of the car but a requirement for the REAR doors (where applicable) is that they latch securely and can be opened from the outside.

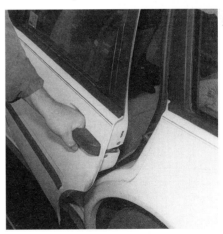

latched securely in the closed position.

❏ SPARE WHEEL CARRIER

If your car has an external wheel carrier (some Citroëns and many pick-ups/vans, for example) it has to be in good condition and securely attached. Positioned under the vehicle where it is at the mercy of the elements and road dirt, corrosion is often a problem. As most people don't have a flat tyre from one year end to another, it could well be rusted solid. Bearing that in

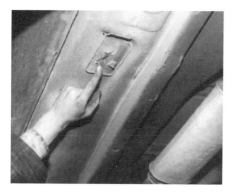

Top: Check seat mounting bolts but if no amount of tightening does the trick, a glance underneath might provide the answer. It could be loose because of corrosion around one or more of the seat mounting areas. If this is your problem, then you must get it welded before the test, otherwise it will definitely fail.

Middle: The seats must be capable of being secured in the upright position. Particularly prone to test failure are two-door/four-seat cars where the front seat back rests have to be pushed forward to allow rear passenger access. Constant use of a period of years can wear the locking mechanism.

Bottom: Incredibly enough, child seats are not part of the test. Having personally witnessed some of the appalling DIY fitting that abounds, I can heartily recommend that any child seat be taken to a professional for fitting or, at the very least, for him to check over your own work. It will cost you a few pounds more, but in many cases, seats are fitted so as to be positively lethal to the child who could end up paying the ultimate, tragic price.

with WD40 or similar and treat any exposed threads to wire brushing and a thick coating of grease.

❏ SEATS
EXCEPTION TO THE RULE

mind, it's a good idea to ensure that it operates correctly and, moreover, is not likely to fall off. Spray any moving parts (hinges etc)

The tester will take into account original design limitations when performing these particular tests. If, like some early VW Beetles, your

The main problems are when the silvering starts to deteriorate (due to the ingress of water behind the glass) and, of course, cracks in the mirror. A small, single crack which does not affect the rearward vision unduly would also probably pass the test, but where the mirror damage is as bad as the one shown here (which had been struck by another car in an accident) then it would certainly fail. Replacing the whole mirror assembly is usually an expensive business, though it's possible to buy 'cut-to-size' stick-on replacement mirrors for a fraction of the cost.

seats have no provision to be secured in the upright position, then it is not a failure point. The tester is checking to ensure that where a locking mechanism is present, it is working correctly.

❏ MIRRORS
HOW MANY & WHERE?
All passenger cars first used after 1st August 1978 and having less than 7 seats must have at least:

One exterior mirror (either door or wing mounted) on the driver's side of the car plus either an interior mirror or an exterior mirror on the passenger's side.

Of course, it is common practice today to manufacture vehicles which have an interior mirror and twin exterior mirrors as a matter of course. It should be noted that the testing procedure only applies to the obligatory mirrors and not any additional mirrors that have been fitted. The tester will first check that the mirrors show a view to the rear of the car, are of the right number, securely mounted and usable.

The basic rule is that the view to the rear must not be seriously impaired, which means that a minor crack on the mirror lens will not

necessarily mean a fail, given that the visibility is still good and that the glass is not insecure.

❏ FUEL SYSTEM
Remember that strict safety rules should be adhered to when dealing with your fuel system. Petrol is highly flammable and so are its vapours, as well as being dangerous to inhale. Let no one smoke in the immediate vicinity, make sure that there is plenty of ventilation and make sure that there is a fire extinguisher to hand.

The tester is, once again, looking to ensure that your fuel system is safe. This means all parts of it, from the petrol tank to the carburettor/ injectors. He is looking specifically for leaks, either in the pipework or at the joins. In addition, the routeing of the fuel lines is important - they should be secure and not passing close to moving items which could conceivably damage them.

The carburettor/fuel injection system should be examined for any leaks. Because of the nature of petrol (it evaporates quickly) a running engine may reveal leaks not previously obvious: see Safety section earlier in this book. Check all

Under the car, the fuel lines must show no signs of leakage. Where there are clips in the bodywork to secure the fuel lines, they must be in good condition and actually in place. In this case, where the clips are undone, it would be a failure point.

pipes and unions and, where applicable, fuel filters (as found on diesel engined cars). Bear in mind that fuel injection systems (especially diesels) operate under high pressure and could cause serious personal injury if mishandled. Make sure you fully understand your particular fuel system before attempting anything other than a basic examination.

Check the whole fuel system for integrity, including in-line filters.

❏ **REGISTRATION PLATES & VIN DETAILS**

The MoT test now includes registration plates (number plates) and the VIN - vehicle identification number - plate.

The accompanying diagram shows the rights and wrongs of number plates. The registration number has to be clearly visible and there has to be one plate at the front of the car and one at the rear. The plates can be square or oblong, something usually dictated by the design of the particular car.

The tester will check that the fuel filler cap (locking or otherwise) is a good, secure fit and that the sealing rubber is in a good condition and not allowing fuel to spill out (for example, when you have a full tank of fuel and are cornering hard). Temporary caps are NOT acceptable.

The rights and wrongs of registration plates.

The trend of recent years of buying 'cherished' numbers and ones which make a word or name, has caused a few problems for owners who fall foul of the law. As the diagram shows, closing up the letters and numbers to make ANN 1E into ANN1E, looks impressive, but only until the 'boys in blue' spot it. And it certainly won't pass the test, which states that the gap between the numbers* and the letters should be at least twice the distance between adjacent digits.

* WHERE A LETTER IS USED AS A SUFFIX OR PREFIX TO NUMBERS TO DENOTE THE MODEL YEAR, IT IS TREATED AS A NUMBER.

EXCEPTION TO THE RULE

Where the vehicle to be tested has never been registered, there is no need for registration plates to be fitted. Any vehicle with foreign or diplomatic registration plates does not have to conform to these standards.

VIN PLATES

Vehicles first used on or after 1st August 1980 (except kit cars and amateur-built vehicles) have VIN (vehicle identification number) or chassis plates

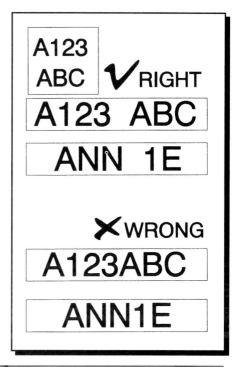

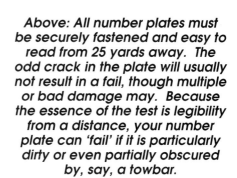

Above: All number plates must be securely fastened and easy to read from 25 yards away. The odd crack in the plate will usually not result in a fail, though multiple or bad damage may. Because the essence of the test is legibility from a distance, your number plate can 'fail' if it is particularly dirty or even partially obscured by, say, a towbar.

Typical European VIN plate.

fitted by the manufacturer and it's an important point to check that the numbers match up with those on the registration document when you buy a used car. The plate can usually be found in a prominent position in the engine bay (sometimes in the door shuts or on top of the dash panel). The VIN plate should be firmly secured to the body and the method of securing (usually rivets) should not obscure the information thereon.

In some cases, the VIN details are stamped into the vehicle chassis or body and, again, they should be clearly legible to the tester.

If you find that your car does NOT have its VIN details either on a plate or stamped, you should contact your nearest Vehicle Registration Office, before presenting your car for the test.

SPOT CHECKS

The fact that your car carries a current MoT certificate does NOT necessarily mean that it is road-worthy - only that it was road-worthy at the time of the test. As such, and in order to provide an incentive for owners to keep their cars in tip-top condition, the police are empowered to 'spot check' vehicles to ensure that they meet certain basic safety requirements.

Your car can be subject to a safety spot check at almost any time though most are carried out in the event of the police stopping you for other purposes (at the scene of an accident for example). You will be required to present a current MoT certificate, either there and then or within seven days at a police station. Regardless of that, there are a number of minimum standards which must be adhered to, viz -

❏ SEAT BELTS
Seat belts must be fitted to the front seats of all cars and the rear seats of some - see chapter 7 for full details. Seat belts must be worn at all times where one is available. The responsibility for wearing the belt lies with the individual except where he/she is a child under 14 years of age, in which case it is the responsibility of the driver to ensure that the child is fully belted-up. All fitted seat belts must be maintained in full working order and must not be damaged or have loose mountings.

❏ HORN
Your vehicle must always have a fully functional horn. It follows that to make sure yours is in working order, you must test it from time to time, but remember the law - it is illegal to sound your horn whilst the vehicle is stationary or between the hours of 11.30pm and 7.00am in a built-up area.

❏ SPEEDOMETER
Your speedometer should be accurate and fully functional. If you are caught exceeding a speed limit, an excuse of 'my speedo wasn't working' will not be enough; indeed, on top of a 'speeding' ticket, you'll end up with another for driving a vehicle in an unroadworthy condition!

❏ EXHAUST
Your car's exhaust system (which includes the downpipe) should be in sound condition and capable of performing the task for which it was meant, i.e. reducing noise, smoke and fumes to an acceptable level. Holes in the system, creating extra noise, for example could mean that your car is illegal. It must also be securely fastened to the car - a tailpipe held in place by a piece of string is unlikely to satisfy any custodian of the law.

❏ TYRES

The basic rule with regard to tyres is that there should be a *minimum* tread depth of 1.6mm over three quarters of the width. However, the rest of the tyre comes in for scrutiny, too. The sidewalls must be free from splits and cracks and there must be no foreign bodies (nails etc.) in the casing.

And don't forget, they must be inflated to the correct pressure - serious under or over inflation not only causes increased tyre wear, it can result in a car that is inherently dangerous to drive.

It is not a legal requirement to carry a spare wheel and tyre (though you've got to be extremely trusting in luck not to) but when you do, the tyre has to comply to the same rules.

❏ WINDSCREEN & WINDOWS

The rule that you should be able to see clearly out of all windows is obvious. But any winter sees any number of drivers peering through a small frost-free circle on the windscreen while they wait for the demister to work. Apart from being illegal, it's incredibly stupid! All cars must be fitted with functioning windscreen wipers and windscreen washers. The washer system should be free of leaks and provide reasonable water jets onto the screen.

❏ LIGHTS

All lights must be in full working order, and that includes side, rear, head (full/dip beam), fog and indicator.

The fact that you are not driving at night when stopped or that (you say) you never drive at night, makes no difference. Your lights must be exactly as required by the law at *all* times.

And finally ...

Your car must have a current MoT and you must be covered by a current insurance certificate. And don't forget that your (valid!) tax disc must be positioned on the lower corner of the nearside (passenger side of a RHD car) of the vehicle.

❏ THE PENALTIES

If you are stopped and faults are found, you could be in for some penalty points on your licence or a cash fine or both. But in some areas of the country (and for some offences) the police are experimenting with a scheme whereby the offender is allowed a short time limit to correct the area of unroadworthiness at the end of which he is required to present the car at a police station to show that

OFFENCE	PENALTY POINTS	MAX FINE
Driving a car without an MoT certificate	0	£1000
Driving a car without insurance	6/8	£5000
Driving a car with defective tyres/brakes or steering	3	£2500
Not wearing a seat belt	0	£500
These figures are correct at the time of writing but are subject to change.		

all is now well. Not doing so by the end of the specified period renders the owner liable to the relevant fine/penalty points.

The table on the facing page shows the maximum penalty points and fines that can be awarded for the respective offences.

THE TEN-MINUTE TEST

You can't give your car a thorough going-over in just ten minutes but, by the time you've booked it in for the test, you should be truly confident it will pass. So, the 'triple T' is your final check-up before you head toward those three blue triangles.

Major items (wheel bearings, brakes, etc.) will have already been sorted in your more thorough MoT preparations and, overall, are not likely to have changed much: if the brake pads were in good condition last week, they'll probably still be so this week. But the rigours of modern motoring are such that a perfectly legal car today could be illegal tomorrow through the smallest, easiest to solve fault: a large stone chip on the windscreen, a headlamp bulb failure or a nail through a tyre could all happen the day before the test.

So, take ten minutes the morning before the test to check the following items - it could save you a lot of hassle and money.

❏ **EXTERIOR**
• Is the car clean? It's easier to see any last-minute faults and you'll go up in the tester's estimation right from the start - no-one wants to crawl about under a car that looks as if it's just been driven through a ploughed field!

• Stand outside the car and check that all the lights operate exactly as they should, front and rear, not forgetting the direction indicators/hazard lights. You'll need a helper to check rear lights/brake lights. Don't forget to tap them gently with your hand to make sure they don't flicker.

• Ensure that none of the lenses are broken or damaged in such a was as to be a failure point (i.e. where they are dangerous or showing white light).

• Check your tyres for foreign bodies and general damage - you'll already know they're legal in terms of tread depth and width from your previous checks. Are they inflated correctly?

• Check that all the locks on the car are satisfactory and can be locked and unlocked on demand; the front from inside and outside, the rear from the outside only.

• Look hard at the windscreen - have any cracks or chips appeared in the past few days? Use the hole-checker mentioned in Chapter 8 to see if any damage will pass the test.

• Take a final look at the windscreen wiper rubbers to ensure they are not damaged or split. Try out the windscreen washers to ensure they are fully operative.

• With the car in the open air, start the engine and walk around listening for noises which could indicate an exhaust leak.

• When you're at the corners of the car, try the suspension 'bounce' test; apply your weight to the corner and then release suddenly. The car should settle down quickly.

• Make a visual check of the bodywork all round the car. You're ooking for anything which could be construed as dangerous to other road users.

• Your mirrors should give a clear view of what's behind. Badly cracked or severely corroded mirrors won't do.

• Your car's number plates, front and rear, should be clean and legible, as should your VIN plate, which is usually found under the bonnet.

• Check your car's fuel cap. It should be secure and the rubber seal in good condition.

❏ **INTERIOR**
• Check that seat belts operate correctly and do not snag on anything.

• Make sure that front and read seat backrests can be secured in the upright position (where appropriate).

• Put your vehicle registration document (V5) and current MoT certificate in the glovebox.

❏ **UNDER THE BONNET**
• Make a visual check for obvious problems, e.g. leaking or split pipes, loose or damaged fittings. Check that both the brake fluid reservoir and windscreen washer bottle are topped up correctly.

At this point I'd usually wish you the best of luck with the MoT test but, of course, if you've studied the rest of the book, and finished it off with the ten minute test, you won't need it!